MESSI

The Inside Story of the Boy who Became a Legend

Luca Caioli

CORINTHIAN BOOKS

An earlier edition of this book was published in 2008 by
10 Books and Columna, Spain and in 2009 by Planeta, Argentina

Published in the UK in 2010 by
Corinthian Books, an imprint of
Icon Books Ltd, Omnibus Business Centre,
39–41 North Road, London N7 9DP
email: info@iconbooks.co.uk
www.iconbooks.co.uk

Sold in the UK, Europe, South Africa and Asia
by Faber & Faber Ltd, Bloomsbury House,
74–77 Great Russell Street, London WC1B 3DA or their agents

Distributed in the UK, Europe, South Africa and Asia
by TBS Ltd, TBS Distribution Centre, Colchester Road
Frating Green, Colchester CO7 7DW

Published in Australia in 2010
by Allen & Unwin Pty Ltd,
PO Box 8500, 83 Alexander Street,
Crows Nest, NSW 2065

ISBN: 978-190685-011-1

Typeset in New Baskerville by Marie Doherty

Printed and bound in the UK by
CPI Mackays, Chatham ME5 8TD

Contents

Chapter 1
Rosario

Present day

'I buy the rump or a piece from the hindquarter. They're cuts of beef I've also seen in Barcelona but I don't know what they're called. I put a bit of salt on each piece, dip them in egg and coat them in breadcrumbs. I fry them until they're nice and golden-brown and I put them in an oven dish. I slice the onion finely and fry it over. When the onion turns white, I add chopped tomatoes, a little water, salt, oregano and a pinch of sugar. And I leave it on the heat for around twenty minutes. Once the sauce is done, I pour it on top of each piece of beef, making sure they're well covered. I take some cream cheese or hard cheese out of the fridge and lay it on top of the beef in thin slices. I leave them in the oven until the cheese melts. All that's left to do is fry the potatoes as a side dish and the *milanesa a la napolitana* [schnitzel napolitana] is ready to serve.'

With the passion and experience of a good cook, Celia describes her son Lionel Messi's favourite dish.

'When I go to Barcelona I have to make it two or three times a week. And with at least three medium-sized cuts of beef. I tousle his hair and tell him: "My schnitzel napolitana and my *mate* [traditional Argentine tea] are what make you score so many goals." It's true: when he scored three against Real Madrid, I was there making his favourite dish and preparing the tea for the evening.' Lionel has simple

1

gastronomic tastes: schnitzel, but not made with ham or horsemeat; chicken with a sauce made of pepper, onions, tomatoes and oregano. He doesn't care much for elaborate dishes, like the ones his brother Rodrigo makes, but then, as is well known, Rodrigo is a chef and his dream is to open his own restaurant sooner or later. It is natural for him to experiment and try new recipes, although his younger brother doesn't always appreciate them. Does he have a sweet tooth? 'Yes, Leo loves chocolates and *alfajores* [traditional caramel-filled biscuits – a national delicacy]; when we go to Spain we have to take boxes and boxes so that he always has a good supply.' She tells the story about how, when he was little, when a coach promised him an *alfajor* for every goal he scored, he netted eight in a single match. Some feast.

Over a cup of coffee in La Tienda bar on San Martín de Rosario avenue, the mother of Barça's number 10 talks with great gusto about the son who is known throughout the world. Black hair, a delicate smile and certain facial features that remind one of Leo (although she laughs and says that he resembles his father completely), Celia María Cuccittini Oliveira de Messi has a soft, gentle voice. While she is speaking, she often glances at her sister Marcela, seated opposite. The youngest of the Cuccittini family, Marcela is also a mother of footballers: Maximiliano, 25, plays for Flamengo in Brazil; Emanuel, 21, has been a midfielder for 1860 Munich, a second division team of the German league, since July 2008; and Bruno, twelve, attends the Renato Cesarini football school, which counts players such as Fernando Redondo and Santiago Solari among its alumni. Marcela Cuccittini de Biancucchi is Leo's godmother and his favourite aunt. When he returns to Rosario, it is in her home that he likes to pass his time. 'We have to go and meet him or call him to see how he is, but, of course, my sister spoils him,' says Celia. 'And then there's Emanuel, they're inseparable.' From a very young age they were continually playing ball. 'There were five boys: my three, Matías, Rodrigo and Leo, and my sister's two, Maximiliano and Emanuel. On Sundays, when we would go to my mother's house, before lunch they all used to go out into the street to play,' recalls Celia. They were wild games, of football or foot-tennis and often Leo would end up returning to the house crying because he had lost or because the older ones had cheated.

'Just the other day, Maxi was reminding me about those games,' adds Marcela, 'and he was telling me that when they all meet back here in Rosario he wants to play Messis against Biancucchis, just like the old times.'

And the memories bring us to the grandmother, Celia: her delicious food, the pastries, the Sunday family reunions and the passion for football. 'It was she who accompanied the kids to their training sessions. It was she who insisted that they let my Lionel play even though he wasn't old enough, even though he was the youngest and he was small. Because,' says Celia, 'he's always been small. They were afraid he'd get trodden on, that he'd get hurt, but she wasn't, she insisted: "Pass it to Lionel, pass it to the little guy, he's the one who scores goals." It was she who convinced us to buy him football boots. It's a shame she can't see him today. She died when Leo was ten years old, but who knows if, from up there, she sees what he has become and is happy for that grandson of hers whom she loved so much.'

But how did Leo begin playing football? From whom did he learn? Where do all his many skills come from – is it a question of genes? 'I don't know, from his father, from his brothers, from his cousins. We have always loved football in our family. I am also a fan. My idol? Maradona. His career, his goals, I followed them with much passion. He was a barbarian on the pitch. When I met him, I told him: "I hope one day my son will be a great footballer and you can train him." And look what's happened ... now Maradona is the national team coach ...'

A pause in the story: the mobile phone on the table starts to ring. Celia excuses herself and moves away to answer it. Meanwhile, Marcela returns to the topic of young Leo. 'He was incredible, before he was even five years old he could control the ball like nobody else. He loved it, he never stopped. He hit every shot against the front gate, so much so that often the neighbours would ask him to cool it a bit.'

Celia has turned off her phone, she sits down and nods in agreement. 'The worst punishment we could threaten him with was: you're not going to practice today. "No mummy, please, I'll be really good, don't worry, I promise ... let me go and play," he begged and insisted until he convinced me. Leo wasn't a temperamental child and he wasn't lazy either, he's always been a good boy, quiet and shy, just as he is today.'

Really? 'Yes, really. He doesn't take any notice of the fame. When he comes back to Rosario he always wants to come and wander around this area, along San Martín avenue, with his cousin Emanuel. When we tell him it's not possible, that here the people of his hometown will get hysterical when they see him and not let him go two steps, he gets upset. He doesn't understand it, he gets annoyed. In Barcelona, he goes to the Corte Inglés [a department store] in his trainers and sports gear. Ronaldinho often used to ruffle his hair and ask him if he was crazy going out dressed like that. He hasn't taken any notice of who he is. That's why being famous, signing autographs or taking photos with fans doesn't bother him. Some evenings, when he comes home after a long time and when I go to see him, I lay by his side on the bed. We chat, I tousle his hair, I tell him things, and

I say, half joking: "What all the girls wouldn't give to be next to you like this." He makes a weird face and says: "Don't be silly mum."'

On the walls of the bar hang the shirts of Argentine players. Leo's is there too, under a window, marked with the number 30 of Barcelona. 'They don't know I'm his mother, although we live in this town,' comments Celia, a woman who shies away from fame, very aware of the risks that come with celebrity, and having clear priorities for her life and those of her children. All well and good, but how does she feel being the mother of a star? 'Proud, very proud. Opening the newspaper and seeing – here just as much as in Spain – a piece about him or seeing his shirt number, or seeing the kids who wear it ... it makes me swell with pride. That's why it hurts me to hear criticism about his playing or false information about his life. It affects you deep down in your soul and it pains you when someone calls you and says, have you seen this, have you seen that? Leo? He hardly reads what they write about him. If he notices it, it doesn't affect him greatly. But that isn't to say that he hasn't been through some tough times. He too has had his low moments, when he was injured, out for months, when things don't go how he wants them to go. At times like that, I don't even think twice, I pack my bags and I go to Barcelona, to see what's happening, to be close to him, to look after him as much as I can. Leo has always been a boy who keeps all his problems inside, but at the same time, he's been very mature for his age. I remember, when we hinted at the possibility of him returning to Argentina, he said to me: "Mum, don't worry, I'm staying, you go, God will be with us." He is very strong willed.'

She returns to the topic of his success, of the people who go crazy for the 'Flea' on both sides of the Atlantic. 'The thing I like the most is that people love him,' says Celia.

'They love him, I think, because he is a simple, humble, good person. He always thinks of others and he makes sure that everyone around him is OK: his parents, his siblings, his nephews and nieces, his cousins. He's always thinking about his family. Of course, I'm his mother and a mother, when she speaks of her children, the apples of her eye, always says good things, but Leo has an enormous heart.'

How does a mother see her son's future? 'In terms of football, I hope he makes history like Pelé, like Maradona, I hope he goes far, very far. But above all, as a mother, I hope to God he will be happy, that he has a family, that he lives life, because he still hasn't really lived. He has dedicated himself to football, body and soul. He doesn't go out, he doesn't do many of the things that young people his age do. That's why I hope he has a wonderful life. He deserves it.'

Outside the large window, the sky has darkened. The traffic has become more chaotic: buses, rickety vans, cars that leave a cloud of smoke behind them, a cart full of junk pulled by a skinny horse and a multitude of people who wend their way to the shops and the bus stops. Celia has to get home; María Sol, the youngest of the family, is waiting for her there. Marcela has to pick up Bruno from football school. It's raining and Celia insists on accompanying her guests back to the centre of town. She goes to fetch the car. At the door, a few last words with Marcela about a mother's fears – injuries, money that can go to one's head. 'For now, my kids, and Leo, haven't lost their sense of reality. I, my family, and my sister's family, we live in the same town in which we were born, in the same house as always, we haven't moved to a different region, we haven't wanted to leave our roots, and the kids are the same as always. I hope they never change. I hope what has happened to other footballers, who have lost themselves in all the fame, doesn't happen to them.'

A grey Volkswagen stops by the pavement. Celia drives rapidly through the streets in the southern part of Rosario. She passes Leo's old school and comments: 'He wasn't a good student. He was a little bit lazy.'

She turns right by Tiro Suizo, a sports club founded in 1889 by immigrants from the Tesino region. Two kids don't notice the car, they are too absorbed, ball between their feet, cantering along.

'That's what Lionel was like,' says Celia.

Chapter 2

Garibaldi Hospital

24 June 1987

A cream-coloured construction built in the nineteenth-century style occupies a rectangular plot at number 1249 Visasoro street. It is the Italian hospital dedicated to Giuseppe Garibaldi, who is also honoured with a statue in Rosario's Plaza de Italia. He is a popular figure, known as the 'Hero of the Two Worlds', because during his exile in South America he fought battles along the length of the Paraná river. In those parts his Red Shirts left their mark wherever they went: for example, in the names of the Rosario and Buenos Aires hospitals, which were founded by political exiles, supporters of Mazzini and Garibaldi, and their workers' unions. The Rosario hospital complex was inaugurated on 2 October 1892 in order to serve the Italian community, which at that time represented more than 70 per cent of the immigrants who had arrived from the other side of the Atlantic. Today it has one of the best maternity units in the city. It is here that the story of Lionel Messi, third child of the Messi-Cuccittini family, begins at six o'clock one winter morning.

His father, Jorge, is 29 years old and is the head of department at steelmaking company Acindar, in Villa Constitución, some 50 kilometres outside Rosario. Celia, 27, works in a magnet manufacturing workshop. They met at a young age in the Las Heras neighbourhood, previously known as

Estado de Israel and today known as the San Martín neighbourhood, in the southern area of the city, where the resi-
dents are humble and hardworking. Celia's father, Antonio,
is a mechanic – he repairs fridges, air conditioning units
and other electrical items. Her mother, also called Celia,
has worked for many years as a cleaning lady. Jorge's father
Eusebio makes his living in construction; his mother, Rosa
María, is also a cleaning lady. Little more than 100 metres
separate their homes. Like many other local families, they
have Italian and Spanish ancestors. The surname Messi
comes from the Italian town of Porto Recanati, in the province of Macerata, which saw the birth of the poet Giacomo
Leopardi and the tenor Beniamino Gigli. It is from there
that one Angelo Messi departed on one of the many boats
bound for America at the end of the nineteenth century, in
search of a better life in the new world, like so many other
emigrants carrying third-class tickets. The Cuccittinis also
have Italian roots, on their father's side. Despite these families originating from the humid pampas, they eventually
came to settle in the city.

At 305 kilometres from the capital city of Buenos Aires,
and with around a million inhabitants, the city of Rosario
is the largest in the Santa Fe province, extending along the
banks of the Paraná river. The Costanera promenade runs
alongside the river until the Nuestra Señora del Rosario
bridge, which crosses the waters and the islands in the
river and connects the city with Victoria. The Paraná has
always been an important highway in the river trade: from
here, many agricultural products are exported to the whole
of the Mercosur – like soya, which, in recent times, has
brought wealth to this region and transformed the area's
urban fabric. New buildings, skyscrapers and incredible vil-
las are springing up in front of a beach of fine sand depos-
ited by the river. And yet, Rosario remains the patriotic city

par excellence. School groups dressed in white pose for photos at the base of the monument of the flag, built in the old Soviet style and inaugurated in 1957 to mark the place where General Manuel Belgrano ordered the raising of the national flag for the first time, on 27 February 1812.

Rosario is a city of the grandchildren of immigrants, of slums and country houses. But let us leave aside the stories of immigration, the mix of cultures, languages and traditions, which are plentiful in Argentina, and return to Jorge and Celia, who fell in love and began dating at such a young age.

On 17 June 1978 they marry in the Corazón de María church. The country is thoroughly absorbed in the World Cup – so much so that the newlyweds, honeymooning in Bariloche, still ensure that they catch the Argentina-Brazil match taking place in Rosario. The result is nil-nil. Eight days later, at River Plate's Monumental stadium in Buenos Aires, César Luis Menotti's sky-blue-and-white Argentine national team, known in Argentina as the Albiceleste (literally meaning 'white and light blue'), beats Holland 3-1 to win the World Cup. Collective mania ensues. Fillol, Olguín, Galván, Passarella, Tarantini, Ardiles, Gallego, Ortiz, Bertoni, Luque and Kempes seem to banish all memories of the Proceso de Reorganización Nacional (period of military rule) – the deceased dissidents and the 'disappeared' (more than 30,000 of them) and the tortures and horrors of General Jorge Rafael Videla's ferocious and bloody military dictatorship, which was instigated on 24 March 1976 with the dismissal of Isabel Perón. On the streets of Buenos Aires you can still see the words 'Inmundo mundial' – dirty world (cup) – painted beneath the green of a football pitch and the inscription '1978'.

Two years after the *coup d'état*, the country is still under a reign of terror, but life goes on. Celia and Jorge become parents: Rodrigo Martín is born on 9 February 1980, and their second son, Matías Horacio, is born in one of the darkest hours of the country's history. The date is 25 June 1982, the Falklands War having ended eleven days earlier. Argentina, defeated, counts her losses (649 dead) and her casualties (more than 1,000), on top of which must be added all those who will never forget those two and a half months that were 'illuminated by fire'. Young, inexperienced and ill-equipped men, volunteers convinced to enlist by a cheap patriotism in order to re-conquer the Falklands archipel-ago, occupied by the British in a distant 1833. Operation Rosario, the name of the key Argentine invasion led by General Leopoldo Galtieri on 2 April 1982, was the ump-teenth attempt at distraction orchestrated by the military junta, intended to divert attention from the disasters of the economic programme introduced in 1980 – policies that had led to 90 per cent inflation, recession in all areas of the economy, a rise in external debt for both private companies and the State, the devaluation of salaries, and in particular the progressive impoverishment of the middle class (a char-acteristic of the country's history which stands out as com-pared with other Latin American nations). The war should have made the country forget the dramas of the past and engulfed the people in a wave of patriotism, but Galtieri was not prepared for the Iron Lady, Margaret Thatcher, nor had he taken into account the British army.

In a few weeks British forces quash the Argentine army – a disaster that will lead to the fall of the military junta and the celebration of democracy within the year. But the restoration of the Malvinas – the Argentine name for the Falklands – to Argentina remains an ongoing demand: in Rosario, in the Parque Nacional de la Bandera (literally, 'national park of the flag'), a monument has been built in honour of 'the heroes that live on the Malvinas Islands', and the 1994 Constitution lists the territory's restitution as an objective that cannot be renounced. In 1983, however, election victory belongs to Raúl Alfonsín, one of the few politicians who had kept his distance from the military, maintaining that their only objective in going to war was to reinforce the dictatorship.

Four years later, when Celia is expecting her third child, the situation is still dramatic. In Semana Santa (Holy Week) of 1987, Argentina is on the brink of civil war. The *carapintadas* (literally, painted faces) – young army officers captained by Colonel Aldo Rico – have risen up against the government, demanding an end to the legal trials against human rights violations committed during the military regime. The military commanders are unwilling to obey the president. The people take to the streets to defend democracy. The CGT (Confederación General de Trabajo – the labour union) declares a general strike. On 30 April, Raúl Alfonsín addresses the crowd gathered in the Plaza de Mayo, saying: 'The house is in order, Happy Easter' – a phrase that will go down in history, because nothing could be further from the truth. With no power over the armed forces, the president has had to negotiate with the *carapintadas*, guaranteeing them an end to the military trials. The law of Obediencia Debida (due obedience) exculpates officers and their subordinates of the barbarities that were committed and deems them responsible only for having obeyed the orders of their superiors. It comes into force on 23 June 1987, the same day that Celia is admitted to the maternity ward at the Garibaldi hospital. Her other sons – Rodrigo, seven, and Matías, five – stay at home with their grandmother, while Jorge accompanies Celia to the hospital. After two boys he would have liked a girl, but the chromosomes dictate that they are to have another boy. The pregnancy has been uneventful, but during the final few hours complications arise. Gynaecologist Norberto Odetto diagnoses severe foetal distress and decides to induce labour in order to avoid any lasting effects on the baby. To this day, Jorge can recall the fear of those moments, the panic he felt when the doctor told him that he was going to use forceps, his plea that he do everything possible to avoid using those pincers, which, as is the case with many parents, concerned him greatly due to the horror stories he had heard regarding deformity and damage to one's baby. In the end the forceps were not needed. A few minutes before six in the morning, Lionel Andrés Messi is born, weighing three kilos and measuring 47 centimetres in length, as red as a tomato and with one ear completely folded over due to the force of labour – anomalies which, as with many other newborns, disappear within the first few hours. After the scare comes happiness: the new arrival is a little bit pink, but healthy.

Outside the confines of the hospital, however, the situation is much less calm. A bomb has exploded in the city and another in Villa Constitución, where Jorge works. Throughout Argentina the number of blasts – in response to the due obedience law – rises to fifteen. There are no victims, only material damage. The bombs reveal a country divided, overwhelmed by military power and entrenched in a grave economic crisis. The secretary of domestic commerce has just announced the enforcement of new prices for basic goods: milk and eggs are to rise by nine per cent, sugar and corn by twelve per cent, electricity by ten per cent and gas by eight per cent – difficult increases for a working-class family like the Messi-Cuccittinis, despite being able to rely on two salaries and a property to call their own. Aided by his father Eusebio, Jorge built the house over many weekends on a 300-square-metre plot of family land. A two-storey, brick building with a backyard where the children could play, and in the Las Heras neighbourhood. Lionel arrives here on 26 June, when mother and son are discharged from the Italian hospital.

Six months later, Lionel can be seen in a family album, chubby-cheeked and smiling, on his parents' bed, dressed in little blue trousers and a white t-shirt. At ten months he begins to chase after his older brothers. And he has his first accident. He goes out of the house – who knows why? – perhaps to play with the other children in the street, which is not yet tarred, and along which cars rarely pass. Along comes a bicycle and knocks him over. He cries desperately; everyone in the house comes running out into the street. It seems it was nothing, only a fright. But throughout the night he does not stop complaining and his left arm is swollen. They take him to hospital – broken ulna. He needs a plaster cast. Within a few weeks it has healed. His first birthday arrives and his aunts and uncles buy him a football shirt, already trying to convince him to support his future team – Newell's Old Boys. But it is still too soon. At three years old, Leo prefers picture cards and much smaller balls – marbles. He wins multitudes of them from his playmates and his bag is always full. At nursery or at school there is always time to play with round objects. For his fourth birthday, his parents give him a white ball with red diamonds. It is then, perhaps, that the fatal attraction begins. Until one day he surprises everyone. His father and brothers are playing in the street and Leo decides to join the game for the first time. On many other occasions he had preferred to keep winning marbles – but not this time. 'We were stunned when we saw what he could do,' says Jorge. 'He had never played before.'

Chapter 3

The smallest of them all

A summer afternoon in 1992

The Grandoli ground is almost bare. A lot of earth and only a few spots of green near the touchline. The goalposts are in a terrible state, as is the fence, as is the building that houses the showers and dressing rooms. The neighbourhood itself is not much better: makeshift carwashes at every junction along Gutiérrez avenue, used-tyre salesmen, signs declaring 'metals bought here' – in other words scrap metals; there is even a piece of cardboard advertising dog-grooming services. And in the background: the popular construction towers, which appear abandoned although they are not; low, little houses, which have lost their charm of yesteryear; vegetation growing between the cracks in the asphalt; rubbish cooking in the heat; men and old folk with nothing to do; kids on bikes that are too small for them. 'People have changed around here', say the oldest of the old folk, adding: 'At night it's scary to walk these streets.' The delinquents have moved in.

At three in the afternoon there is hardly a soul about. The football pitch is deserted. The kids from the neighbouring schools, who come to play sports at the Abanderado Mariano Grandoli Physical Education Centre number eight (named after a volunteer in the 1865 war who gave his life for his country), have already left and the footballers don't arrive before five o'clock. The only person around is a teacher, in a white t-shirt, blue tracksuit and trainers. He points the way, 150 metres or so, towards the home of señor Aparicio, Lionel Messi's first coach.

Aparicio opens the door with wet hands – he is preparing a meal for his blind wife, Claudia, but he invites his guest to enter and make himself comfortable. Four armchairs, an enormous white dog and a certain musty odour occupy a sparse lounge dominated by an old television. Salvador Ricardo Aparicio is 78 years old, with four children, eight grandchildren and four great-grandchildren; he has a worn face, with the shadow of a moustache, his body twisted like barbed wire, his voice and hands shaky. He has worked his whole life on the railways. As a youngster he wore the number 4 shirt for Club Fortín and, more than 30 years ago, he coached children on Grandoli's 7.5 by 40 metre pitch.

He has nurtured hundreds and hundreds of children, including Rodrigo and Matías. The eldest Messi was a speedy and powerful centre forward; the second played in defence. Grandmother Celia accompanied them to training every Tuesday and Thursday. And one summer afternoon, Leo came with them.

'I needed one more to complete the '86 team [of children born in 1986]. I was waiting for the final player with the shirt in my hands while the others were warming up. But he didn't show up and there was this little kid kicking the ball against the stands. The cogs were turning and I said to myself, damn ... I don't know if he knows how to play but ... So I went to speak to the grandmother, who was really into football, and I said to her: "Lend him to me." She wanted to see him on the pitch. She had asked me many times to let him try out. On many occasions she would tell me about all the little guy's talents. The mother, or the aunt, I can't remember which, didn't want him to play: "He's so small, the others are all huge." To reassure her I told her:

"I'll stand him over here, and if they attack him I'll stop the game and take him off."'

So goes señor Aparicio's story, but the Messi-Cuccittini family have a different version of events: 'It was Celia who forced Apa to put him on when he was one short. The coach didn't like the idea because he was so small. But his grandmother insisted, saying: "Put him on and you'll see how well the little boy plays." "OK," replied Apa, "but I'm putting him near the touchline so that when he cries you can take him off yourself."'

Regarding what happens next there are no disagreements. Let's return to the old coach's narrative: 'Well ... I gave him the shirt and he put it on. The first ball came his way, he looked at it and ... nothing.'

Don Apa, as he's known around here, gets up from his chair and mimics little Messi's surprised expression, then sits back down and explains: 'He's left-footed, that's why he didn't get to the ball.' He continues: 'The second it came to his left foot, he latched onto it, and went past one guy, then another and another. I was yelling at him: "Kick it, kick it." He was terrified someone would hurt him but he kept going and going. I don't remember if he scored the goal – I had never seen anything like it. I said to myself: "That one's never coming off." And I never took him off.'

Señor Aparicio disappears into the other room and returns with a plastic bag. He rummages through the memories of a lifetime. Finally he finds the photo he is looking for: a green pitch, a team of kids wearing red shirts and, standing just in front of a rather younger-looking Aparicio, the smallest of them all: the white trousers almost reaching his armpits, the shirt too large, the expression very serious, bowlegged. It's Lionel; he looks like a little bird, like a flea, as his brother Rodrigo used to call him.

'He was born in '87 and he played with the '86 team. He was the smallest in stature and the youngest, but he really stood out. And they punished him hard, but he was a distinctive player, with supernatural talent. He was born knowing how to play. When we would go to a game, people would pile in to see him. When he got the ball he destroyed it. He was unbelievable, they couldn't stop him. He scored four or five goals a game. He scored one, against the Club de Amanecer, which was the kind you see in adverts. I remember it well: he went past everyone, including the keeper. What was his playing style? The same as it is now – free. What was he like? He was a serious kid, he always stayed quietly by his grandmother's side. He never complained. If they hurt him he would cry sometimes but he would get up and keep running. That's why I argue with everyone, I defend him, when they say that he's too much of a soloist, or that he's nothing special, or that he's greedy.'

His wife calls him from the next room; señor Aparicio disappears and returns to recount more memories.

Like that video that he can't seem to find, with some of the child prodigy's games – 'I used to show it to the kids to teach them what you can do with a ball at your feet'. Or the first time Leo returned from Spain and he went to visit him. 'When they saw me it was madness. I went in the morning and when I returned it was one o'clock the next morning. We spent the whole time chatting about what football was like over there in Spain.' Or that time when the neighbourhood organised a party in Lionel's honour. They wanted to present him with a plaque at the Grandoli ground, but in the end Leo couldn't go. He called later to say 'Thanks, maybe next time.'

The old football teacher holds no bitterness; on the contrary, he speaks with much affection about the little boy he coached all those years ago.

'When I saw on TV the first goal he scored in a Barcelona shirt I started to cry. My daughter Genoveva, who was in the other room, asked: "What's wrong dad?" "Nothing," I said, "it's emotional."'

Aparicio pulls another gem from his plastic bag. Another photo of the little blond boy, shirt too big, legs too short; in his hand he is holding a trophy, the first he ever won. It's almost as big as he is.

Leo is not yet five years old. And in the Grandoli ground he is already starting to experience the taste of goals and success. In the second year, he is even lucky enough to have his old man as his coach. Jorge accepts the offer from the club's directors and takes charge of the '87 team. They play against Alfi, one of their many fixtures across the city. And they win everything: 'But everything, *everything*: the championship, the tournaments, the friendlies ...' recalls Jorge Messi, with more of a paternal pride than that of a coach.

Apart from football, there is school. Leo goes to school number 66, General Las Heras, at 4800 Buenos Aires street. He is accompanied by either his mother Celia, his aunt Marcela, or by the neighbour Silvia Arellano, mother of Cintia, his best friend. They go on foot, making their way across the open country or skirting the edges of the football fields on the grounds of the army barracks of the Communications Batallion 121. In little more than ten minutes they are at the door.

Today, when approaching the entrance, the youngest class can be seen absorbed in drawing. Two of them are wearing Messi shirts. In the enormous covered pavilion, some kids in white kit are playing a match with incredible concentration. There are goals – what's missing is the ball – a bundle of brown paper held together with tape serving instead. They move at a giddying pace, without taking too much notice of the harsh ground of grey gravel – slaloming, feinting, dribbling. Among the players is Bruno Biancucchi, Leo's cousin. Sweating profusely and red from the effort, his charcoal-black hair matted against his face, wearing a white-and-pink-striped earring, his companions soon mark him out as the best. The press has already dedicated a substantial number of articles to hailing him as Leo's successor. His coaches say that he weaves really well, that he has the same talent as his cousin. And, like him, he is shy. The only thing he says is that he envies his cousin's initiative and ability to score goals. Bruno is also a striker and he would like to wear a Barça shirt one day.

A circle of children has gathered. They all want to give their opinion about the boy who until a few years ago went to their school. For Pablo, age eleven, there is no doubt whatsoever: 'He has what it takes to be the best in the world. Better than Maradona. The thing I like best about him is his speed, he's incredible.' Something is worrying Agustín, age nine – something that concerns many of his fellow countrymen – 'Maradona started out at Argentino Juniors, Messi ... at Barça'. Without question, too far away from here. Even the girls, who are more embarrassed, end up joining the group. And here, opinion is divided. Some think he's good-looking, others think he is too short.

It's break time, and under a crooked old piece of wood – an ancient tree – the little pupils chase one another around. Leo used to dodge round the enormous trunk running after paper or plastic balls. For him, the most wonderful memories of those years are precisely those games with whatever object found its way between his feet. He has no problem admitting that he didn't enjoy studying.

And Mónica Dómina, his teacher from first to third grade, confirms that fact: 'No, Leo didn't do so well in his studies, but his work was of an acceptable level. At the beginning he had difficulty reading, so I advised his mother to take him to a speech therapist. In the other subjects he managed to improve little by little, although he didn't obtain wonderful results. He was a quiet child, sweet and shy, one of the shyest students I have seen in my entire teaching career. If you didn't address him, he would sit silently at his desk, at the back of the classroom. The older children competed with him in order to play in Rosario's inter-school tournaments. He was good, of course – he used to win trophies and medals; but I never heard him boast about playing well and scoring goals.'

Chapter 4

The same as always

Conversation with Cintia Arellano

She has bright blue eyes, fine facial features and a slim figure. She is training to be a teacher of disabled children. Only a few more exams and she will be finished. She lives at 510 Ibañez passage, a modest house, where she receives her visitor in a friendly manner. A black dog wags its tail and studies the new arrival before leaving the bare living room and going out into the courtyard that backs onto the Messi family courtyard. Cintia has always been Leo's friend. 'Our mothers were "womb sisters",' she says. Silvia Arellano became pregnant around the same time as Celia. 'We kept each other company,' Silvia explains. 'We would go shopping together and we chatted about the future of our children. It was my first. We were good friends.' She puts a glass of soda on the table and retires, leaving the story to her eldest daughter, who is 22 years old and who went to nursery, infant school and primary school with Lionel, always going to, and coming home from, school together, as well as to birthdays, parties and matches.

What was Leo like when he was little?
'He was a typically shy child and he talked very little. He only stood out when he played ball. I remember that at break time in the school playground the captains who had to pick the teams always ended up arguing because they all

wanted Leo, because he scored so many goals. With him they were sure to win. Football has always been his passion. He often used to miss birthday parties in order to go to a match or a practice.'

And what was he like at school?
'We called him Piqui because he was the tiniest of all of us. He didn't like languages or maths. He was good at PE and art.'

They say you used to help him ...
'Yes, sometimes ... In exams he used to sit behind me and if he was unsure about something he would ask me. When the teacher wasn't looking I would pass him my ruler or my rubber with the answers written on it. And in the afternoon we always used to do our homework together.'

Then later, in secondary school, your paths separated and Leo went to Barcelona ...
'We all cried that summer afternoon when he and his family left for Spain. I couldn't believe it, I was losing my best friend. When we would speak on the phone we would get very emotional and it seemed to me that living over there in Europe was very hard for him. But when he returned we chatted and I realised that it was a very important experience for him, it helped him to mature a lot. It put a strain on his family, so much so that Celia and María Sol came back. He told me that he integrated because there were kids his age who played football. And for him that was fundamental. He wanted to be a footballer and he's made it.'

Cintia gets up, and returns with a folder full of photos and newspaper cuttings. There the two of them are as babies: Leo with a dummy and a blue bib; behind them, an enormous doll dressed as a bride; next to him, Cintia, in nappies and pigtails. And there, at infant school in 1992, in the class photo, all of them dressed in blue uniform. Dressed up for the carnival, him in a policeman's helmet with a fake moustache, her made up, with huge glasses and a white dress. And then there are numerous newspaper pages: 'The new Maradona', 'Waiting for the Messiah', 'What planet have you come from', until we reach the headlines of July 2005, the victory in the FIFA Under 20 World Cup.

'I was the one who organised the party here in the neighbourhood. We went round all the neighbours and asked for money to buy confetti, firecrackers and paint. We wrote "Leo, the pride of the nation" in white letters on the ground, and we put up a banner in his street that said "Welcome champion". He was supposed to arrive at one in the morning, the whole neighbourhood was waiting for him, it was winter, there was a bitter cold and he didn't arrive. Some people got tired and went home. We stayed there waiting until five in the morning, when a white van turned into the street beeping its horn. At that moment all the television cameras were switched on. People started to scream, people were throwing firecrackers, playing the drums and yelling: "Leo's here, Leo's here." He was exhausted. He wasn't expecting such a reception, but it made him really happy.'

Yet more cuttings and more photos of Leo, as well as some tough pages full of criticism after the Argentina-Germany match at the 2006 World Cup, after that image of Leo sitting alone on the bench.

'They said that he was impulsive, that he didn't integrate into the group. They killed him. But it's not like that. Only someone who knows him knows what he feels. When he's not doing so well Leo is a little bit solitary, he retreats, he withdraws into himself. He was like that even with me sometimes. It was like drawing blood from a stone trying to find out what was going on inside. But for me above all, Leo is a smile.'

And he hasn't changed?
'No, to me he's the same as always, shy and quiet. He's the same Leo with whom I grew up. The only difference is that before when he used to come here he would grab his bike and come through town; now he takes the car because people don't leave him in peace. He can't believe the madness he generates. The same people from his neighbourhood now take photos of him, the girls wait outside his front door to say hello to him. The boys want to be like him. It surprises and amazes me when I hear what they scream in Spain or when he plays with the national team. So when someone asks me about him, I usually prefer to keep quiet. I don't want them to think I'm gossiping or trying to get myself noticed. No, for me Leo is a humble, lifelong friend, who still has no idea that he is so famous.'

Chapter 5
Red and black

21 March 1994

Raúl: 'I've always been surrounded by good Argentines like Valdano, who gave me my debut at Real Madrid, or Redondo, or the team-mates with whom I now share a dressing room. I have a great relationship with all of them. I wish I could go to Argentina sometime soon and enjoy some football over there. I want to see a Boca or a River match.'

'Or Newell's,' adds Lionel Messi in a low voice.

'The Flea' does not miss a single opportunity to reaffirm his red-and-black passion. To the extent that even while in conversation with the Real Madrid captain as part of a publicity event, he ends up bringing up the team he loves. It is to be expected – Newell's is a family love. His father Jorge played there from the age of thirteen until he began his military service. A midfielder with a great eye for the game, more defensive than attacking, although he never made it to professional level. Rodrigo joined their football school aged seven and Matías followed in his footsteps.

Leo arrives directly from Grandoli in early 1994. The club scouts know about him. They have asked his brothers to bring him along to find out if he really is extraordinary, which is how the youngest Messi brother ends up playing eight games in as many different formations in the minor leagues, during afternoons and evenings over the course of almost a month for the club. It is an intense test and he does not disappoint. The Newell's coaches think he is phenomenal and recommend him for the Escuela de Fútbol Malvinas (Malvinas School of Football), which nurtures particularly young players. He is not yet seven years old. The club's directors have to consult with the parents first, but given their family passion for football there is no problem.

'The father came to see me and said to me: "I'm going to take him to Newell's,"' recalls Salvador Aparicio, the old Grandoli coach. 'What could I say to him? Well ... take him then!'

And so, on 21 March 1994, Lionel Andrés Messi, ID number 992312, becomes a member of Club Atlético Newell's Old Boys.

Newell's and Rosario Central are the two rival clubs who divide the passion of the *Rosarinos* (people from Rosario). The Club Atlético Rosario Central was founded on 24 December 1889 as the Central Argentine Railway Athletic Club. It was founded by the English workers who were employed on the railway line. Its first president was Colin Bain Calder. Later, with the merging of the Ferrocarril Central Argentino and the Buenos Aires Railway companies in 1903, the club's name changed. From then on it was to be the Club Atlético Rosario Central. Its colours: blue and gold. Great players have worn that shirt, like Mario Kempes, Luciano Figueroa, José Chamot, Cristian González, Roberto Abbondanzieri, Roberto Bonano, César Delgado, Daniel Díaz, Daniel Pedro Killer, Juan Antonio Pizzi and César Luis Menotti, to name just a few. Two notable fans? Ernesto 'Che' Guevara, who was born in Rosario on 14 June 1928 and whose first home was an apartment at 480 Entre Rios street. A few blocks away, there is a Ricardo Carpani mural in his memory, in the city's Plaza de la Cooperación. And the unforgettable Roberto 'El Negro' Fontanarrosa, one of Argentina's greatest football cartoonists and writers, among other things, who sadly passed away in 2007.

Newell's was founded on 3 November 1903 by the teachers, students and alumni of the Argentine Commercial Anglican school that Kent-born Isaac Newell founded in Rosario in 1884. According to legend, it was he who introduced the first leather ball and the official football rules into the Latin American country. The students at his school – among them his son Claudio, the club's promoter – began to play ball and created the club. From there the name Newell's Old Boys was born, in honour of the father and the school. Its colours: black and red.

One of the things that makes the hackles stand up on the back of the necks of their Rosario Central 'cousins' is having seen Diego Armando Maradona wearing the club's shirt, albeit only for five official matches and two friendlies. It was 1993 and the 'Golden Boy' was back from Europe, where he had begun in Barcelona, moved to Napoli and ended up finally at Sevilla. Aside from Diego there are many other illustrious names, from Gabriel Batistuta to Jorge Valdano, from Abel Balbo to Maxi Rodríguez, from Sergio Almirón to Mauricio Pochettino, from Juan Simón to Roberto Sensini, from Jorge Griffa to Walter Samuel, from Américo Gallego to 'Tata' Martino. The nickname given to the fans? The lepers. Strange, but true. A derogatory epithet that ends up becoming a strong and recognised symbol. This deserves an explanation, and indeed one is offered by a Newell's fan website which is dedicated to more than 100 years of footballing history.

According to what our grandparents told us – which coincides with what is claimed to be popular legend – many years ago the women's beneficiary committee of the Carrasco Hospital wanted to arrange a charity match in aid of 'Hansen's disease', commonly known as leprosy. The match was to be played between Rosario's two biggest teams, so the authorities of both clubs were approached for their approval in order for the match to go ahead. Newell's immediately accepted the invitation, but it was met with a flat rejection by the Central team, making this historical event the first sign of trouble with the Gold and Blues. So it was that Central became the city scoundrels, and this was the main reason for mocking on the part of the Red and Blacks, who gloated over their time-honoured rivals. The Central crowd argued that if Newell's were so interested in playing this particular game, it must be because they were lepers – and it was from here onwards that the Newell's fans became known as 'the lepers' and those of their Central rivals as 'the scoundrels'. Even though this has become the most widespread version of the story over the years, and perhaps is the only true version of the facts, it is worth pointing out that some of the older Rosario generation recount a different explanation of why, according to them, the Newell's fans were always known as the lepers, even before the founding of the club in the early twentieth century, when it was no more than a Rosario educational establishment. According to their version, the issue centres around the fact that in those days it was unusual for houses in the Rosario neighbourhoods to be separated by big dividing walls, which meant that people could talk to their neighbours simply by standing on tiptoe or by standing on a bench next to the aforementioned wall. On the other hand, in those days, this meant that leprosy devastated a substantial part of the population, and Rosario was no exception. This illness, which dates back to biblical times, has always been characterised by the fact that no matter who the sufferer was, they were quarantined out of sight and out of contact with others. Perhaps for this reason, when passing in the vicinity of Mr Isaac Newell's school and upon noting the enormous and apparently impenetrable wall that surrounded it, people were inclined to comment that all the leprosy victims must surely be quarantined out of sight behind it. And so, according to these particular folk, the Newell's Old Boys have been known ever since as the lepers.

It is a nickname that will also be associated with Lionel when Rosario's *La Capital* newspaper interviews him for the first time. But that is still six years away, six more minor leagues and almost 500 goals before Messi will be accorded the honour of appearing in the local press.

Faded red-and-black murals. 'The force of the lepers' written on a fist painted on the fence, the work of some hooligan fans. Above the railings is the banner: 'Escuela de Fútbol Malvinas Newell's Old Boys'. The pitch is in a sorry state, but the children playing there are unfazed. The club's coaches have come to hold trials so they have to do well at all costs. Next to the dressing rooms, a rusty bed lies abandoned in a corner. On the other side, along the Vera Mujica avenue, there are another two pitches in the same state of abandon. Someone comments that the income made from season tickets and ticket sales, and in particular from the sale of so many players to foreign clubs, has not been invested here, in the school where the younger generations are trained. It's patently obvious. Although the truth is that it was not much different when Lionel played his first season in his red-and-black shirt. Perhaps back then there was simply more enthusiasm – more people who worked hard and less money going into the directors' pockets. But let us leave that to one side and talk about that year that started so well and ended with a 3-0 defeat against Tiro Suizo. The boys lost the title, but they learned from their mistakes, given that in the following four seasons they suffered one defeat, this time at the hands of their training mates, the Newell's C team. Thanks to that unstoppable run, the team ended up earning the club the glorious name *la Máquina del '87* – the '87 Machine. The greatest source of satisfaction for Leo was a dolphin, the trophy won at the Cantolao international tournament held in Lima, Peru, in 1996. More than 25 teams from Argentina, Chile, Ecuador and Colombia participated. But in the end it was Newell's who emerged triumphant. And little Messi captured the attention of the media with, among other things, his tricks with the ball. During training and before matches, he would play 'keepy-uppy' for his own amusement. It is a skill of his that even the club's most senior directors appreciate, to the point that he is soon asked on various occasions to entertain the public during the half-time break of the first team's matches. They would announce Messi's name over the speakers and he would go down through the stands doing tricks and then position himself in the centre of the pitch, where he would perform wonders with the ball. It is a half-time that many lepers still remember – their first image of the boy who would one day become Leo Messi.

'He was something special,' recalls Ernesto Vecchio, Messi's second coach at Newell's, from among old American cars in his mechanic's workshop. 'He had wisdom, he could sprint, his passes were spot on, he played for his team-mates, but he was capable of going past half the opposing team. Once on the Malvinas first pitch, the goalie passed him the ball in defence and he ran the length of the pitch and went on to score an incredible goal. He didn't need to be taught a thing. What can you teach to a Maradona or a Pelé? There are only very tiny things for a coach to correct.'

There are so many memories of those two years, from age nine to eleven, when Vecchio coached Leo. Like the Balcarce tournament, for example, where the Newell's '87 team knocked out teams like Boca, Independiente and San Lorenzo. Lautaro Formica, a defender in that particular team, maintains that they had nothing to do because 'the ball never came back in our direction. I remember that Rodas and Messi created havoc between them. Once Messi had the ball, the opposition would get out of the way. Sometimes those of us at the back got quite bored.'

Gustavo Ariel Rodas, aka Billy, the other star of that team, is the antithesis of Leo. Or, to put it another way, the proof that possessing a natural talent does not guarantee success. Billy, an attacking midfielder from the '86 team with extraordinary technical abilities, is also from Rosario but was born in a shanty town. At fourteen he was a substitute in the Newell's first team and he had his first child. Before his sixteenth birthday he debuted in the first division and everyone predicted a bright future. Today, at 22 and with two children to call his own, he is lost to oblivion. 'It happens to many players who come from the slums, from poverty,' explains Vecchio. 'Football helps them escape their misery, but afterwards, if it doesn't suit them, they return to the slum, they fall into alcohol, drug use, desperation. Education is the definitive difference. In Leo's case, he has a father and mother who have supported him and helped him become what he is today. I believe very strongly in family environment as one of the factors in a footballer's success.' Ernesto Vecchio still has time for one more anecdote, the most juicy of all: 'We were playing against Torito, a club from our league. Leo was sick and I didn't want to make him play. I kept him on the bench. There were only a few minutes left before the final whistle and we were losing 1-0, so I went over to Leo and I said: "Do you fancy playing?" He said yes. He warmed up and just before he went on I yelled to him: "Win me the match!" And he did – in five minutes he netted two goals and turned the score around.' Nothing out of the ordi-

nary seeing as, between championships, tournaments and
friendlies, the Flea scored around 100 goals a season.

In 2000, the tenth league is the last that thirteen-year-old
Leo plays in with the '87 Machine, under the direction of
Adrián Coria. They win it at the Bella Vista ground, where
the first team trains. And it is then that, on 3 September,
just two weeks before his departure for Barcelona, *La
Capital* prints the first interview, a double-page spread:
'Lionel Andrés Messi, a little leper who's a real handful.'
The introduction goes something like this: 'He is a tenth-
division player and he is the team's playmaker. As a boy he
is not only one of the most promising junior lepers, but he
also has a huge future ahead of him, because, despite his
height, he can go past one, past two, beat all the defenders
and score goals, but above all, he has fun with the ball.'

And next, a barrage of questions. Here are just a few of
his answers:

Idols: my father and my godfather Claudio
Favourite players: my brother and my cousin
Favourite team: Newell's
Hobby: listening to music
Favourite book: the Bible
Favourite film: *Baby's Day Out*
Possible career: PE teacher
Objectives: to finish secondary school
Aims: to make it into the first team
Happiest moment: when we became champions of the
   tenth league
Saddest moment: when my grandmother passed away
A dream: to play in the Newell's first team
A memory: when my grandmother first took me to play
   football
Humility: is something a human being should never lose
What Newell's means: everything, the best.

Chapter 6
He was a Gardel

Conversation with Adrián Coria

The television is on. Images of the Shakhtar-Benfica match fill the screen. On the table, the computer is running. Adrián Coria, ex-Newell's player and ex-coach of the lepers' youth teams, is on vacation but he is working from home. He is the assistant coach to Gerardo 'Tata' Martino, manager of the Paraguayan national team, and his job is to keep an eye on Paraguayan nationals like Oscar Cardoso. But it is always a pleasure to recall one of his ex-players.

Let's begin with your first impressions when you saw him play.
'At that time there was a lot of talk about Leandro Depetris, a little blond boy who went to Milan aged eleven. Everyone was saying wonderful things about him. I disagreed. I always used to say to a friend of mine: "Leo will be ten times better than Depetris. When he grows up he'll be greater than Maradona – and I'm a huge fan of Diego."'

How could you be so certain about predicting such a great future for a twelve-year-old boy?
'When you saw him you would think: this kid can't play ball. He's a dwarf, he's too fragile, too small. But immediately you'd realise that he was born different, that he was a phenomenon and that he was going to be something impressive. Why? Because he was explosive, he had a command

34

that I had never seen on a football pitch. He's Formula One, a Ferrari. He anticipated the next step, he had moves – one-on-one he'd make mincemeat of you. He dominated the ball, always on the ground, always glued to his foot. He left behind all the big boys who still didn't have good control of movement and coordination. He was 1.2m tall. He dazzled against central defenders of 1.8m. He made a huge difference. And he had a strong temperament – he was competitive, he liked to win. I have never seem him resign himself to any result. He wanted to win every game.'

What position did he play?
'Behind the strikers. I used a 4-3-1-2 formation; with me, Lionel always played freely or in the hole. During a match it was impressive to watch him pick off his opponents. The others wanted to take him down, they knew of his abilities and they tried to stop him. He'd get kicked at from all sides. But him ... nothing. He never complained. On the contrary, it seemed that fouls spurred him on, the more they went for him, the more he stood up to them. He would go after the ball and within a few moments he was already in front of goal. He won matches all on his own, so much so that they used to say to me: "You don't direct this team when Leo's on the pitch."'

Any goal or match that stands out in particular?
'There were goals of all different types. Matches? With him we won them all. He was a Gardel [in other words, a legend, like the famous tango singer Carlos Gardel].'

Did he listen to the advice of the coach?
'Yes, he was respectful. He paid attention. He never said "I'm playing", he never said "I'm the best". His team-mates adored him. The only thing was ... he didn't like exercises. He loved the ball. That's why I once had to send him off during training. I'm not an ogre or a sergeant major, but I've

always liked people to take things seriously. We were doing a lap, and he kept playing around with the ball. I called to him once, twice, but it was like he took no notice ... Finally I said to him: "Give me the ball, get changed and go home." Ten minutes later I saw him with his bag on his shoulder, glued to the wire fence, watching the pitch. I felt bad and it saddened me to see him like that. "You left without saying goodbye," I yelled over to him. He came over to say goodbye and I sent him back to the changing room so that he could rejoin the practice. He was a shy kid with a tough character, but that was the only time I had to say something to him.'

What did you think when he went to Spain?
'That Newell's didn't take a chance on him, they didn't make enough of a financial effort, they didn't want to spend money on a thirteen-year-old kid. I think they didn't realise the value of what was right in front of them.'

And now, what do you think of him?
'It seems to me that he has grown an enormous amount in Europe – in terms of football. But he still hasn't reached his full potential.'

Fame, celebrity, money ... can they detract from the game?
'I think fame has helped him grow, because he knows how to use his head. And he hasn't changed. He is still the same humble boy. I ran into him recently. We were just finishing our training, they were starting. He saw me. He left the warm-up. He came over to say hello and gave me his shirt. My players couldn't believe it and they asked me if they could meet him, or if I could ask him for another shirt.

'That's just one example. It had been a while since I had seen him ... but he seemed to me to be the same kid who trained at Bella Vista.'

Chapter 7
Size: small

31 January 1997

Doctor Diego Schwarsztein remembers precisely the date of the first appointment: 31 January, his birthday. That was the day he met Lionel. He was nine and a half, and his parents, concerned about their third son's limited growth, had brought him to the doctor's consultation room at the Clinic for Glands and Internal Medicine, number 1764 Córdoba street, in central Rosario.

'It was a consultation about small stature, of which I do many each day,' recalls the doctor. Leo measured 1.27m; he was not a star, he was not a renowned footballer, nor even a professional, he was just playing junior football at Newell's. 'And I have always been a lepers fan [to prove it, there is a picture of his son underneath the glass on his desk, at a match where the Red and Blacks scored a goal against Boca]. This helped me to establish a good rapport with the patient. We used to talk about football, the only topic of conversation that would conquer the little boy's shyness.'

Numerous appointments, more than a year of investigation, complex tests, biochemical analyses and clinics. 'Because only tests can determine if we're dealing with a hormonal problem or if it's simply a case of finding ourselves up against what is usually known as a "late bloomer" – a child whose growth rhythm differs from that of his contemporaries, who develops later.'

To clarify, the doctor points out the significant dates and time periods in a clinical history, indicating the normal periods which are necessary in these cases in order to reach a diagnosis: growth hormone deficiency.

The explanation: 'The glands aren't making any growth hormone,' says Schwarsztein. 'To make a readily understood comparison, it's a case analogous to that of a diabetic, whose pancreas does not produce insulin. In this case, we're dealing with the substance needed in order to grow. The difference is that diabetics represent seven per cent of the world's population, whereas Messi's case is not very common: it affects one in every 20 million, according to statistics. And it's worth noting that it's not hereditary. Just look at Leo's brothers, or María Sol, his little sister, who is decidedly tall.' How did Leo deal with this news? 'I remember,' says the doctor, 'that he had a very healthy relationship with his illness; he dealt with all the tests – even the most invasive ones – and the therapy, without too much trouble. His family helped him a lot with that – a first-class family.'

Once the problem was identified, the endocrinologist began a programme of growth hormone treatment. One subcutaneous injection every day for anywhere between three and six years, until the patient has developed sufficiently.

How can the development be evaluated? How can one measure the potential for growth? With an x-ray of the hand. The doctor shows them at different stages of development: age nine, ten, eleven, up to eighteen years old. He points out the blank spaces between one bone and another and explains that when these disappear it means that the patient has reached their potential – they will not grow any more. Then he adds: 'Nothing allows us to overcome genetics, but if difficulties arise we can help it along. I should emphasise that those who genuinely have growth hormone deficiency have it for life. That's why it is necessary to intervene.'

In the case of Messi, this definitely was not some kind of experiment. He was not, as someone has written, a lab rat. The doctor loses his patience and says emphatically: 'It was never an experiment. For many years growth hormone has been used in such cases, more than 30 years in fact. It used to be extracted from cadavers, but there was a risk of CJD. Since the mid-1980s it has been produced through genetic engineering. The long-term side effects are not confirmed. But we haven't had any problems in any of our cases so far – like in Messi's case, where it is imperative that we replace what is lacking.'

So, why are growth hormones such a taboo subject, and why is it one of the most commonly used products when it comes to drug taking among sportsmen?

'Administered to an adult without a deficiency, in other words to a person with a normal level of secretion, growth hormone serves as an anabolic steroid to increase muscle mass and decrease fat tissue. It increases physical output and performance,' explains the doctor. But the risks to one's health are extremely high: it can trigger anything from liquid retention to hyperthyroidism, from high blood sugar levels to cranial hypertension, and there is also a risk of tumours.

Despite having dealt with suspicions and fears, in both Argentina and Spain, there remains an issue about which much has been written – although generally without rhyme or reason – namely the cost of treatment, which can amount to 600,000 Argentine pesos a year (roughly equivalent to £100,000). It is a considerable sum, which may well have pushed the Messi family to depart for Spain, since Barcelona was the only club willing to take care of the expenses.

'It always caught my eye, the story in the media that the father took the footballer away because they wouldn't pay for the treatment here. It's not definite that they didn't want to pay here. The father's social security took care of the treatment, along with the Acindar Foundation. It's not certain that they had to leave the country for that reason. Because here, if the parents have social security or medical insurance the treatment is approved by the Programa Médico Obligatorio [Compulsory Medical Programme] and if they don't have cover, there is the National Advisory Committee for Children with Growth Hormone Deficiency which has administered free treatment since 1991.'

It's a version that contrasts with that of the Messi family. According to Jorge, the father, the medical insurance and the Acindar social security stopped paying the total cost of the treatment after two years. Seeing the child's promise, the Newell's authorities initially agreed to cover part of the costs (every other injection). But little by little, the payments began to arrive late. 'We went so many times to ask for the money, that in the end my wife said to me: "I'm not going to ask any more." And that's what happened,' says Jorge, who did everything he could to find a solution to the problem.

'River had opened an office in Rosario. It was a chance for the boy, and also a way of putting the pressure on Newell's. We went to Buenos Aires for a trial. Leo trained in Belgrano and during the first match, when they brought him onto the pitch, they realised what he was worth, that he wasn't just some little kid. "We want him," they told me,' recalls Jorge Messi, '"but only if you bring us the paperwork, if you can get Newell's to agree to let him go." In other words, they didn't want to get into trouble with Newell's. So nothing was done about it. Newell's found out about it and they asked me not to take him away. They made other promises. Then along came Barcelona ...'

With the matter more or less cleared up, there is one fact about which the Messis and Schwarsztein agree: 'The hormone deficiency and its treatment are nothing more than an anecdote – what really matter are the boy's football-ing skills.' And here, getting up from his chair and pacing around his study, the doctor unleashes a series of reflec-tions of a man passionate about football. He speaks with great fervour about the quick sprint; about control of the ball; about speed; about 'Leo's limits, which nobody can pinpoint; the *porteños* [Buenos Aires locals] who are jealous of a player who has hardly set foot in the capital, because here, in order to be successful, it's imperative that you play for one of the big Buenos Aires teams. Look at Batistuta – he was from Newell's, but he only became famous in Argentina when he went to Boca.'

Let us leave football aside for a moment and take a step back. The growth hormone treatment might be anecdotal but look at how a recent article has appeared in *La Capital* entitled 'They want Messi's drug for their children'. The body of the article reads as follows: 'Ever since the therapy given to Messi became public knowledge, for many peo-ple the growth hormone has been transformed into the "magic drug" that makes little children grow. Small stature is a huge concern for parents, especially when children are starting infant school and they are compared with others. Comparison is never healthy, because the normal rate of growth is extremely varied. In the majority of cases, small stature is due to genetic factors, malnutrition in the first two years of life, or a delay in development or growth (for which there is no specific therapy), but many parents are demanding from their paediatricians the same treatment given to Leo Messi.'

'These are the negative consequences of media divul-gence regarding a therapy associated with a famous footballer, and the erroneous interpretation that parents and the population in general have made,' protests the doc-tor. 'None of this would have happened if everything had remained within the confines of doctor–patient–parent confidentiality. My duty is to insist that this particular course of medical action will do nothing for children who do not have the hormone deficiency, especially taking into account the costs against the lack of benefits. But it is imperative for those who do suffer from the deficiency, as Lionel does. That's why he started receiving the treatment in 1998, when he measured 1.27m; and after continuing with the treatment in Barcelona, he now measures 1.69m. Without this cure he would not have grown to his genetically intended height.'

Chapter 8

International star in a small town

Conversation with Mariano Bereznicki,
La Capital journalist

What does Leo Messi represent for Rosario?
'The best player the town has ever produced. Argentine hope. He is a footballing icon. We are all waiting for the day when he becomes Diego's successor.'

How is he known around here?
'In Rosario he isn't "known". He played junior football. He only played here until the tenth league. He didn't become popular. Only those who came up against him on the pitch saw him. Some of us have heard about that time, when Leo was already promising in the short term, and herein rests the nightmare of the Rosario clubs: they didn't realise what they were losing. That's Leo's unfinished business, never having played here. He's a product of Newell's. Sooner or later we hope to enjoy seeing him on our pitches. At the moment we can only see his talents on television when he plays with Barça, or in Buenos Aires if we head over to the Monumental de Núñez stadium or wherever the national team are playing.'

When did you first meet him?
'At the end of 2000. Leo was returning from Barcelona. I interviewed him without any problem. We went over to the

monument of the flag to take some photos. People didn't recognise him. He was little, just like everyone else. My impressions? A very submissive kid of few words. But he's like that, he transforms when he steps onto the pitch, he changes completely when the ball is at his feet. On the pitch the real Lionel Messi appears. You have to sit back and enjoy it.'

Five years later everything changed ...
'It was after the 2005 Under 20 World Cup. That's when Messimania began. It was all the rage. The media mobbed his house: newspapers, TV channels, national and international radio stations. Everyone wanted to interview him, talk to him. And so did the locals. Not a day passed when someone didn't come up to him to congratulate him or ask for his autograph. Why such a frenzy? Because Argentina had been waiting for someone like him for a long time. They were talking about Riquelme, Tévez, Aimar ... and along came Messi. He surprised us all with what he did at that World Cup. He proved himself as a distinct class of footballer – unique. And he was crowned King of Holland.'

And now when he comes to Rosario, what happens?
'When he comes here he's an international star in a small town. Because he has signed deals with important, internationally renowned firms, he represents capital. The companies need to promote him and people want to see him. But he takes refuge in his family, and his friends ... in order to return strengthened and in the right frame of mind for his demanding Barcelona life. Rosario is where he can recharge his batteries.'

In your opinion, what is he really like, this famous Rosarino?
'Only his intimate circle knows the real person. Even after reading many things about him one cannot really know him. It's not easy. It seems to me that he is painfully humble. Stardom is not drowning him, it hasn't changed him. He's as solid as a rock.'

And in terms of football?
'I think he was born from a mould that had seemed long forgotten since Maradona.'

Let's analyse his skills.
'Solidarity with his team, loyalty, attacking with the ball, and with dynamite possessed by few others. His power to accelerate is impressive. And he does all this in a unique way.'

And the future? What do you predict?
'Leo's future has already arrived. He has proven himself now in the competitive game of Spanish and European football. But he is still very young. He hasn't reached his maximum level of explosiveness, although he has certainly scored some outstanding goals that are comparable to Diego's.'

Is he the new Maradona?
'He is the true Messi.'

Chapter 9

Across the pond

17 September 2000

English	Spanish (Spain)	Spanish (Argentina)
goalie	*portero*	*arquero*
bus	*autobús*	*colectivo*
Danish pastry	*bollo*	*factura*
biro	*bolígrafo*	*birome*
flip-flops	*chanclas de dedo*	*ojotas*
apartment	*piso*	*departamento*
skirt	*falda*	*pollera*
round (in shape)	*esférico*	*redonda*
t-shirt	*camiseta*	*remera*
coat	*abrigo*	*sobretodo*

... and in Spain, the word *coger* means 'to get' or 'to catch', while in Argentina it means something altogether more vulgar, which is best left unmentioned.

They say that the same language is spoken in Spain and Argentina and, in effect, the language of both countries is *castellano* – literally, Castilian, denoting standardised Spanish – but the differences are numerous, and not just in terms of the meaning of particular words or expressions of slang (charming or otherwise). It is a question of different ways of life and, on occasion, different ways of understanding life. Almost all Argentine families have some Spanish or Italian ancestors, but more than a century after great-grandfather left the Iberian peninsula, or the Italian boot, becoming a *gallego* (slang for Spaniard) or a *tano* (slang for Italian), things have changed significantly. History has opened up a chasm, creating profoundly different cultures, such that today, if one abandons the current path and returns to the country of origin, adapting is no mean feat. It is always a difficult challenge: more so if the one who must face it is a boy of barely thirteen. It requires much willpower to leave behind one's childhood, one's hometown, school, friends, the team that one loves, the Malvinas and Bella Vista grounds, and part of one's own family. And, above all, without any guarantees for the future.

Leo Messi and his father Jorge leave Rosario for Barcelona on 16 September 2000.

Let us take a step back and find out why father and son are embarking on an Aerolíneas Argentinas transatlantic flight, how they came to the decision to try their luck on Catalan soil, and what they are expecting from their journey.

At thirteen years of age Leo is already a well-known figure in youth football. The newspapers dedicate double-page spreads to him, he is talked about in the minor leagues, and even in Buenos Aires his game has been very positively evaluated by River Plate. Two years previously, Fabián Basualdo, former defender for both Newell's and River, represented Leo for a number of months, attempting to direct his career as well as possible, until the Messi family realised that it was unnecessary for someone so young to have an agent. But one fine day in 2000, Martín Montero and Fabián Soldini, of Marka – a company with Rosario headquarters dedicated to the buying and selling of players – introduce themselves at number 525, Estado de Israel. Lionel's father Jorge does not want to speak about these people, because as the story unfolds it is revealed that they did nothing to help his son

– in fact they did rather the opposite ... such that there are lawsuits and appeals in various court cases even today. Legal disputes aside, let us continue with the story.

Montero and Soldini want to represent Lionel. They are convinced that the young lad could have a bright future with any great team, be it in Italy or Spain, from Inter to Milan, from Real Madrid to Barcelona. They make assurances that they have contacts and friends in high places. The Messis do not succumb easily to empty promises. Until the boy manages to land a trial in Europe, no one is going to take care of the bills.

It did not seem to be an impossibility, given the precedent set by Leandro Depetris, the boy who had gone to Europe to train with the Milan youth team. The only thing to do was to see if these friendships and contacts were not simply a ruse. They were not: in August 2000, Montero and Soldini call Horacio Gaggioli, one of their associates in Barcelona. Gaggioli, a Rosarino who has been buying up real estate in Barcelona since the 1970s, works with the football agent Josep Maria Minguella, Barça shareholder number 2292, transfer advisor to then president Joan Gaspart, and future candidate in the elections that resulted in Joan Laporta becoming club president.

'I saw a home video of the lad; Horacio, Martin and Fabían assured me that it was worth me taking a look. So I called Charly, who is a good friend of mine,' recalls Minguella.

'He told me about a really good kid ... Something like Maradona. I thought he was talking about a boy of eighteen or nineteen – when they told me his age I was surprised,' adds Carles (also known as Charly) Rexach, who was the technical director of FC Barcelona at the time. 'He'd have to be absolutely phenomenal for us to take an interest. It wasn't club policy to sign kids from outside Catalonia, let alone a non-EU player. They assured me there was no one else like him. I travelled quite a lot in South America, but we decided to bring him to Barcelona to train with us over a few weeks so that the coaches at the club could have the chance to watch him at their leisure. That was the best solution; it was better for him to come to Spain with his family when it suited him than for us to plan a trip to Argentina. Anything could have happened – he could have been ill, or unable to play that week ... For us to go over there would have been unhelpful.'

And so on Sunday 17 September 2000, Lionel arrives in the capital of Catalonia accompanied by his father and Fabián Soldini. Horacio Gaggioli is waiting for them at El Prat airport to take them to the Plaza Hotel, in the Plaza de España at the foot of Montjuïc, where years later Leo would debut with the first team in the Olympic stadium. The city can be seen from the windows of the hotel: if things go well, if there is a place for him at Barça, this will be his new home. There will be a house, money, a job for his father and maybe even a team for his older brother, Rodrigo.

It seems strange that an entire family should put all their faith in a thirteen-year-old boy. Before they got married, Celia and Jorge had already thought of emigrating to Australia – they wanted a new life in a new world. Things were not bad, but they knew they could not achieve much more. Their life in Argentina could not change for the better. They were looking for a new opportunity for their children, and Leo could receive his medical treatment in Barcelona and continue to improve his football at a great club, as his talent deserved. But it was not an easy decision. The Messis asked themselves time and again whether or not they were doing the right thing. Before leaving, they gathered the family around the table and asked each one of them what they wanted to do, making it clear that if even one of them did not want to go, they would all stay in Rosario.

The trial is arranged for the afternoon of Monday 18 September. Leo is stunned by all the sporting facilities. He makes them take a photo of him behind one of the gates of the Miniestadi (the reserve and youth team stadium), just like the multitude of tourists who visit the Nou Camp every day. Then he goes into the dressing room to change and joins the youth teams on the second and third grounds. During the course of a week he trains and plays a short match with children his age. Jorge watches in silence from the stands, just as he always used to do at the Rosario grounds. Not wanting to disappoint his father, Leo scores five goals and another, which is disallowed, all in a single match. Dad had promised to take him to buy a tracksuit if he managed to score six. In the end he has to keep his promise.

All the coaches who see him comment that the Argentine kid plays very well, but it is Rexach who must make the decision regarding his future. Charly is on the other side of the world, in Sydney, Australia, where the Olympic Games are taking place. He has gone to observe the football tournament, which will conclude with a Spain-Cameroon final, eventually won on penalties by the Africans. And so, Leo's stay in Barcelona is extended until his return, scheduled for 2 October. The matter has been left up in the air and needs to be resolved as soon as possible, so a match is organised between cadets, aged fourteen–fifteen, and first-year students at the Miniestadi third ground on Tuesday 3 October at 5.00pm. Charly wants to see how Leo fares against older lads.

'I was coming straight from a meal and I arrived at the ground five minutes late. The two teams were already playing,' recounts Rexach. 'I had to run halfway round the pitch to get to the bench where the coaches were. It took me seven or eight minutes to get all the way round. By the time I sat down on the bench I had already made my decision. I said to Rifé and Migueli [the youth team coaches]: "We have to sign him. Now." What had I seen? A kid who was very small, but different, with incredible self-confidence, agile, fast, technically polished, who could run flat out with the ball, and who was capable of swerving round whoever stood in his way. It wasn't difficult to spot it; his talents, which are now known to everyone, were more noticeable at thirteen. There are footballers who need a team in order to shine – not him. To those who tell me that I was the one who discovered Messi, I always reply: if a Martian had seen him play they would have realised that he was very special.'

The boss has agreed; the deal is done. Two days later, Leo and his father are on a flight to Buenos Aires. They return home happy. Via a third party, Charly Rexach has assured them that they will soon be invited back to Barcelona so that the details of the contract can be formalised. To this day, Jorge does not know Charly personally, although he agrees that the fact that his son plays for Barcelona is thanks to the coach's stubbornness.

The adventure on the other side of the Atlantic has gone well. But in the final stages things do not turn out to be so easy. There are still many difficulties to overcome. Today, Rexach – who is known as the Pedralbes Kid, one of the most emblematic figures of Barcelona FC – recalls all the issues precisely, over a coffee in the bar of the Princesa Sofía Hotel, a stone's throw from the Nou Camp.

'First of all, he was foreign, and the law doesn't allow a foreign child to play in any national league. A considerable handicap. Second, he was a kid. He could end up not becoming a Barcelona player, whether due to his own choice, injury, or age. Third, what are his parents going to do? We'd have to find work for them if they moved to Spain. And

finally, the boy has a growth problem, he needs treatment.'
Rexach explains that he weighed up the pros and the cons,
and he was convinced that they had to take a risk no matter
what 'and sign him, because he's so good'. Nonetheless, not
everyone at the club is so convinced and when the moment
comes to make a decision, questions arise. Some see Leo
as being too small and scrawny and think that this is just
about a nifty little player. Charly responds immediately
to such objections: 'Bring me all the nifty little players, I
want them all in my team.' Even the club president, Joan
Gaspart, wants an explanation of the matter, asking if it is
worth them taking on the responsibility of the family of a
thirteen-year-old boy. And Charly says yes, it is a necessary
risk. Meanwhile, time ticks on. October and November pass
by without the anticipated decision having been reached.
On 4 December Minguella calls Rexach. They meet in the
restaurant of the Pompey Real Tennis Society, in Montjuïc.
Horacio Gaggioli – who at that time represented the Messi
family – is also present. He is the most insistent: 'Charly,
we've got this far. Either you play him or the boy goes elsewhere ...' Gaggioli remembers adding: 'I wasn't bluffing.
We had already begun talks with Real Madrid.'

'They didn't trust me, they didn't trust Barcelona. They
wanted a written agreement or that was the end of the negotiations,' says Rexach. 'I knew for sure that I couldn't let that
kid slip through our fingers, so I grabbed a paper napkin
and wrote something to the effect that the club promised to
sign Leo Messi if the agreed conditions were met. I signed
it and I gave it to him.'

Both Minguella and Gaggioli also signed the paper napkin (a relic which has been conserved with care), an agreement of honour that is, nonetheless, insufficient. Before
packing all their bags and leaving for Barcelona, the Messis
want some guarantees. Starting with the cost of the jour-

ney and extending to the house and a job for Jorge, who will have to leave his job at Acindar in order to follow his son and the rest of the family. Charly Rexach works hard to resolve the problems, but it is not easy. 'At the beginning we couldn't discuss a contract. He was a kid who was going to play youth football, but it was a signing that had to be made, and we made it.'

On 8 January 2001 a final agreement is reached in Via Veneto, another Barcelona restaurant. Joan Lacueva, then director of professional football, meets with youth academy coordinator Joaquím Rifé, who is looking towards the future and wants the club to make an effort to woo Messi. And he asks for a report from the enthusiastic Rexach, who simply writes that Messi is incredible. Two letters are therefore written to Jorge Messi: one from Charly, who confirms the sporting agreement made with the family in Barcelona, and the other from Lacueva regarding the financial terms. In it he includes details of the house they are to rent, the school, and the 7 million pesetas (approximately equivalent to £40,000) the footballer's father would receive as remuneration for a position at the club, which is as good a way as any of remunerating the footballer himself, who would only have been entitled to a study grant.

The letter is enough to convince the Messis to pack their bags. On 15 February 2001, in the depths of the Barcelona winter, the entire family touches down at the Catalan airport.

Chapter 10
Latigazo

Conversation with Fernando 'Chiche' Niembro,
Fox TV commentator

Let's talk about Messi and his transfer to Spain.
'He didn't stop in, or even pass through, Buenos Aires. Ezeiza, the international airport where he departed for Europe, is not even in the city. He went as a kid with growing problems and in Barcelona he exploded. We knew nothing about him. The Spaniards pinched him from us, and then we found out that there was a left-footed kid over there who was doing really well. What happened then happens more frequently now. The big European clubs recruit very young South American players. They don't need to have played in the first league or be champions in order to be bought. They extract them by helicopter from a Brazilian slum and put them in their football schools. It's an exodus of talented youngsters that damages our leagues.'

How would you assess Messi now?
'Messi is currently a *latigazo*.' [Literally 'lash', or 'crack of the whip'.]

What does that mean?
'He is a destabilising footballer, he can shake up a whole game with a single action. There are good footballers who are unable to do that over 90 minutes, whereas he's capable

54

of enthusing the crowd and his critics with a single dodge, a single feint. But we Argentines aren't used to that. We're used to great players who are the whole package, coordinated, who give their talent to the service of the team; that's what Messi still has to learn.'

What does he have to learn?
'He needs to understand that he is part of a whole, he has to share the ball, pass it more quickly, give the final pass and not just make it him versus the whole world. Because sometimes he gives the impression that he wants the ball all for himself and he doesn't want to share it. He has time to learn and he needs a good teacher and great team-mates. And he has them: in a great institution like Barcelona.'

Anything else he needs to learn?
'He should be wary of marketing.'

In what sense?
'He should never be thinking: if I don't have a good game I won't sell watches, or soft drinks, or whatever.'

Changing the subject … Messi and Maradona?
'The comparison is inevitable because Maradona and Pelé are footballing paradigms, but it's unfair. The comparison will be made at the end of Messi's career, but it will never be correct.'

Why?
'Because today's players have more obstacles than twenty years ago. Football is faster and more physical. There are more matches, and there's more information. We know everything about everything; it's difficult for there to be surprises and exceptions. It's a more complicated world.'

Yes, but aren't there some similarities between the two?
'Of course, some features are the same, like the speed or the quick dodge, but Messi's is always in the same direction, whereas with Maradona you never knew if he was left- or right-footed.'

Will Messi supersede Maradona?
'I hope he's better than Maradona. It would be good for Argentine football, but first Messi needs to be champion of the world.'

What does the future hold for Messi?
'It's difficult to predict because the world of football is accelerating at a very dynamic rate. It moves at an incredible speed. Everything changes and evolves in a frenetic way.'

Chapter 11
Provisional licence

6 March 2001

The photo on his first Barcelona ID badge shows him with a plump face and a quiff. And a smile – that was soon to disappear because during the first few months of his new life on Catalan soil, things do not go very well for Leo. On 6 March, a few weeks after his arrival, the Federación Catalana provides him with a provisional players' licence and the next day he is able to debut at the Amposta ground wearing the number 9 Blaugrana shirt (Catalan for 'blue and claret'). He even scores a goal. But he is a foreigner and cannot play in any national competitions, which means he cannot join the children's A team, which should be his team: instead he has to make do with the children's B team, which plays in the Catalan regional league. To make matters worse, by March the teams are already formed and competing, and although he is good, it would be difficult – and unfair – to sacrifice one of the kids who has been playing since the beginning of the season in order to give Leo a place.

Another thing: Newell's is not willing to make the necessary transfer arrangements so that Barcelona can enrol him in the Real Federación Española de Fútbol (Spanish Football Federation).

And that's not all – there is worse still to come. On 21 April a Tortosa defender tackles him hard: he suffers a fractured left leg. It is the first injury in Leo's career. First he needs a splint, then a plaster cast and finally rehab – he won't be able to play again until 6 June.

A week later it happens again. Another injury, this time while walking down the stairs – torn left ankle ligaments. Luckily this injury is less serious – he is out for three weeks.

The only good news on the medical front comes from all the tests and x-rays he was subjected to by the endocrinologists and the club medics. After studying his medical history and growth problems thoroughly, they decide that it is possible to wean him off the growth hormone treatment very gradually. A personalised exercise programme and controlled diet should help the youngster achieve a normal growth rate. Although, ultimately, he will still have to put up with daily injections for a few more years.

As for the rest, his Barcelona experience has started off on decidedly the wrong foot. So much so that by the end of the season, between one thing and another, Leo has only played in two official fixtures and one friendly tournament (excluding training matches). Add to that all the other problems that Leo and his family have had to face and things couldn't really get much worse.

In brief: after staying at the Rallye Hotel, the Messi family move into an apartment on Carlos III avenue – so far so good. Adapting to the new school and new study programmes is more complicated. Leo is enrolled in the Joan XXII state school, in the Les Corts neighbourhood near the Nou Camp. He is still a child who has very little desire to study (he will not achieve level four of his obligatory secondary education, due to his increasingly numerous footballing obligations, among other reasons). Nonetheless, he does not create any problems for his teachers. He is serious, polite and always remains quietly in his corner.

If he manages at least to deal with the situation, by contrast the youngest in the family, María Sol, does not manage to acclimatise to the new way of life.

During the Spanish summer vacation, when they reunite again in Rosario, the family weigh up their options and reach some decisions. Jorge and Celia (who has had to return early to be with her sister, who has undergone an operation) decide that María Sol and the boys should stay in Argentina. They ask Leo what he wants to do. Does he want to return to Barcelona or go back to his old life in Rosario? The boy has no doubt in his mind. He makes it clear that he wants to succeed in Barcelona, there is no need to worry about him. And so, only five months after their arrival, the family is forced to divide in two. On one side of the ocean, Celia, María Sol, Matías and Rodrigo; on the other, Jorge and Leo.

The situation becomes even more difficult than predicted for Leo, who returns to Barcelona on 20 August, now fourteen years old. Summer is over, school and training are starting again. The transfer from the Argentine Football Association is not forthcoming, meaning that he can only play in tournaments and friendlies. There is nothing he can do except put maximum effort into his training sessions and direct all his energy and hope into the friendlies that he plays. It is an attitude noticed by the coaches and his cadet B team colleagues.

Luckily, transfer season begins at the end of the year and continues in the beginning of 2002. In December, Leo's father signs his second contract, which supersedes the one signed in May and helps straighten a few things out – at least from a financial point of view, given that the family situation is not too wonderful due to late payments and bureaucratic problems. In the course of a few years, Leo will sign six contracts committing him to Barcelona FC, which, on the one hand, is testament to his incredible progression as a foot-baller; and on the other to changes in priorities and internal conflicts at the club. There are many such examples: from the director who gets annoyed because he has not been informed of the negotiations and throws the contract in the bin, to the one who would not stand for one kid costing the club so much money. Finally, in February, the FIFA documents arrive, allowing the Spanish FA to arrange Leo's signing. And on 17 February 2002, almost a year after his arrival in Barcelona, Leo is permitted to enter the championship. He plays against Esplugues de Llobregat at the Can Vidalet ground. Messi only comes on after half-time, but adds three gems to the final scoreline of 1-14. Little more than a month later, on 29 March, Leo wins his first Barça title. With much elation, they win the league thanks to a 6-0 victory over El Prat. The bad days are over and the successes keep coming: the Thaygen tournament in Switzerland, and most importantly, the Maestrelli Trophy in Pisa, Italy, from 27 April to 7 May. The B team defeats everyone from Inter to Chievo to Brescia, they draw with Juventus and they knock out Parma in the final. Leo is crowned player of the tournament and suddenly finds his voice ...

'At first we thought he was mute,' says Arsenal captain Cesc Fàbregas, who was his team-mate at the time. 'Then, thanks to PlayStation and that trip to Italy, we discovered that he knew how to talk.'

'Until that moment,' recalls Víctor Vázquez, another of the B-team champions, 'he would always return to the dressing room, sit down in a corner, change, and leave without a word. In Italy he began to gain confidence.' Particularly with Víctor, who nicknamed him 'dwarf'. To get back at him, Leo would respond in *lunfardo*, Argentine slang. It was impossible to understand him. Coach Tito Vilanova agrees that the Maestrelli Trophy was an opportunity for Messi to spend time with his team-mates, get to know them and overcome his shyness. 'Because he wasn't timid at all on the pitch,' says Vilanova. 'When he played it was like watching Maradona when he was his age.'

He gained not only the praise of his coach, but also the respect and sympathy of his peers. The 2001–02 season, which had not begun all that well, ended magnificently at home and away. In the end, victories over Madrid and Espanyol in the Villarreal and San Gabriel tournaments were the icing on the season's cake.

By the 2002–03 season he was in the A team: 30 league games (he was the only player to play in every game), 36 goals (five more than Víctor, the striker), three hat-tricks, one four-goal match, and two titles (the Liga de División de Honor and the Copa Catalunya). And that was without counting trophies like the Ladislao Kubala Memorial Trophy, or the summer triangular tournaments.

Facts and figures help to summarise and evaluate the campaign begun by Leo at his mere fifteen years. He measures 1.62 metres, weighs 55 kilos and is the smallest on the team (the tallest, Gerard Piqué, measures 1.91m), although not quite the youngest (Ramón Massó Vallmajó does not turn fifteen until October). But he is a fundamental part of this talented team, led by Álex García. The only time he is unable to shine is during the Campeonato de España Cup. Neither he nor Frank Songo'o – son of Jacques, the ex-Cameroon goalkeeper from Metz and Deportivo de La Coruña – is able to play (although he still celebrates the victory with the others), because the rules state that only those born in Spain or with a Spanish ID card can play in this particular tournament. An issue which causes many problems and headaches in years to come.

Chapter 12

Puyol's mask

Conversation with Álex García

The appointment is at the Nou Camp ice rink. The young professionals are playing. On the other side of the glass separating the cafeteria and the sports facilities can be seen some difficult exercises and one or two rather inelegant collisions. Álex García knows one of those exercises very well, albeit on a very different type of surface. At 39, he has a career as a midfield goal-scorer under his belt (he debuted in blue and claret on 5 December 1990, in the most famous team of all, the Dream Team), as well as nine years as a coach for the Barça youth team. He is the only one to have coached Messi for an entire season.

Let's go back to the 2002–03 championship.
'It was my second year as an A-team coach. I had a very talented group of kids. I had Cesc Fàbregas, Piqué, Víctor Vázquez and Leo ...'

What was he like?
'Very receptive, always attentive to everything, quiet, shy, reserved, with great class. He was a different type of player, when he got the ball he was unstoppable, he had a devastating sidestep. He would get annoyed on the pitch if you didn't pass it to him, or if he didn't do as well as he wanted,

but he never argued over a referee's decision or over a foul.'

And what was he like with the rest of the group?
'Well, they looked after him a lot, they defended him because he was like their little brother and because the opposition always pounded him, so Piqué or Víctor would always be by his side. Everyone knew he was important to the team, that at any moment Leo could seal a match.'

And has he ever had any problems with you?
'No, he really hasn't. I knew that he was far from home, from his family, that he lived here with his father. I could imagine his nostalgia; sometimes I asked him about it, but he acted like nothing bothered him. He held everything inside. At fifteen years, Leo already knew what he wanted, he was conscious of the fact that he had an opportunity at Barça, he knew what it meant to make a sacrifice – both his sacrifice and his family's, and he didn't want to waste the opportunity he had been given. In terms of football, the only thing that displeased him – he never said anything but you could see it in his face – was playing out of position. I moved him all over the pitch so that he could develop all his skills. It was almost a given in the youth teams. So I played him as a midfielder, sometimes as a centre forward, or on the right or left wing. But he didn't like it. Within a few minutes he would drift towards the centre behind the strikers. You couldn't stop him.'

What can you teach to a kid like that?
'I think he has introduced us to the street football style, "playground football", as they say in Argentina – the dodge, the feint. We in turn have tried to instil in him our attacking kind of football, the Barça kind – getting the ball a lot,

playing as hard as we can, going forward in only two or three touches, driving the ball towards the centre of the pitch and then pushing forward through the opposition's half. Every player should be able to show off his talent.'

The best memory of that year ...
'There are many images of Leo going round in my head but the most incredible story is definitely the one about the mask.'

Let's hear it.
'It was the last game of the league: Barça-Espanyol at the Miniestadi. We only needed a draw to become champions. We were winning 1-0, when all of a sudden Leo clashed with a parakeet [Espanyol] defender. He lost conscious-ness momentarily and he was taken to hospital in an ambu-lance. They said he had a fractured cheekbone. Two weeks' recovery. He couldn't play in the Copa Catalunya, which was only two weeks later. The news saddened the whole team, who had just beaten Espanyol 3-1 and been crowned champions. Well ... the first week passes and in the second the Barcelona medics tell us that Leo can train if he wears a protective mask. Two months earlier, first-team member Carles Puyol had suffered a similar injury and he had opted to wear facial protection rather than undergo surgery. We went to find the mask to see if Messi could use it. The med-ics agreed to it and allowed him to play in the final on 4 May wearing the mask.'

What happened in the final?
'The match begins and after two plays I can see that Leo is lifting up the mask a little bit. It doesn't fit him, he can't see. After two minutes he comes over to the bench and yells at me: "Here's the mask, boss," and he throws it at me. "Leo,

if you take it off I have to take you off the pitch," I tell him. "I could get into a lot of trouble, and you ..." "No, please coach, leave me on a little bit longer," he says. In five minutes he gets the ball twice and scores two goals. The first time he gets it in the middle of the pitch and dodges round the goalie; the second one is a cross from the touchline from Frank Songo'o, which he finishes beautifully. We were 3-0 up at the end of the first half and I said to him: "You've done what you had to do for your team, you can rest on the bench now."'

It's a lovely story. But tell me truthfully, did you ever imagine that Leo would make it this far?
'Not so quickly, no. I was convinced that Messi had a lot of talent and that he'd make it to the first team – but an explosion like that? No. Everything has happened very quickly. That's why I believe that if he doesn't suffer from any serious injuries, Leo will leave his mark on a whole era.'

Chapter 13

Debut

The Dragão stadium is beautiful. Blue, contrasting with the green of the pitch; an open structure that allows a glimpse of Porto all lit up. The white cover closes in the space and provides a view of the pitch. Manuel Salgado's construction, which seats 52,000, was built in order to replace the old Das Antas ground, as well as to house Euro 2004. The inaugural match between Portugal and Greece was held here. It is the backdrop against which FC Porto usually play – a beautiful location and well floodlit for the debut with the first team. Particularly since the date in question is Sunday 16 November 2003, the day of the stadium's inauguration. The crowds have gathered, curious to see a new footballing moment for the city, to experience its magic directly, to wager whether or not the home colours will bring them luck, and to spend half an hour with their eyes trained on the sky admiring the golden blaze of fireworks.

For once, the match is perhaps of lesser importance. A bit of football, very few emotions, a decidedly boring fixture, which, in keeping with the script and to the delight of the home team, ends with a 2-0 victory to Porto.

Lionel Messi debuts in the 74th minute. He is the third substitution for Barcelona, invited to take his place as one of the protagonists of this Portuguese fiesta. This Barcelona team has been obliged to look to youth team players to fill the teamsheet. The internationals have been called up to their respective countries, occupied elsewhere in the Euro 2004 qualifying rounds or in friendlies. So there they are, the promising youngsters, called upon for a trip to Portugal: Jorquera, Oscar López, Oleguer, Márquez, Fernando Navarro, Xavi, Ros, Santamaría, Gabri, Luis García, Luis Enrique, Expósito, Thiago, Jordi, Oriol Riera and Messi, who had scored three goals for the youth A team at Granollers the previous day.

Leo replaces Navarro; he is wearing number 14. And he cannot wait to show what he is worth. So much so that he makes himself noticed in the fifteen minutes he is on the pitch by creating two scoring chances. At the final whistle, Frank Rijkaard comments that 'he is a boy with a lot of talent and a promising future'.

Leo is sixteen years, four months and 23 days old. In the club's history, only two players younger than that have worn the Barcelona first team shirt: Paulino Alcántara – who debuted against Català on 25 February 1912, aged fifteen years, four months and eighteen days – and the Nigerian Haruna Babangida – who was brought on by Louis Van Gaal to play for a few minutes against the AGOVV in 1998 during a pre-season match in Holland, aged fifteen years, nine months and eighteen days. This is undoubtedly a good sign for the young boy who arrived from Argentina two-and-a-half years ago.

In any event, the magical night in Porto is, for the time being, an isolated incident, an exception. Messi will have to wait until the July 2004 Asia tour in South Korea, Japan and China before wearing the first team shirt again.

In the meantime, Barcelona Football Club has seen many changes. On 15 June 2003, Joan Laporta wins the election and becomes the new club president. Frank Rijkaard arrives to preside over the dugout and, on 21 July, Ronaldinho is presented as the new Messiah to 30,000 people at the Nou Camp.

After the *annus horribilis* that was the 2002–03 season (knocked out of the Champions League by Juventus in the quarter-finals; brought down by the Novelda 2nd B team in the Copa del Rey; sixth in the league, 22 points below the champions, Real Madrid; two coaches, Van Gaal and Radomir Antic, and two presidents, Joan Gaspart, and Enric Reyna in the interim), the club's shareholders hope that things will improve and that they will recover the lost ground with regard to their historic Madrid rivals. They need a change of direction. And the changes come. Not only in the first team, but also in the youth teams. Joaquím Rifé is dismissed from his position as football director, and along comes Josep Colomer who, during his tenure, appoints Ángel Guillermo Hoyos as the youth B-team coach, class of 1987. He is an Argentine winger who has played for Talleres Córdoba, Gimnasia y Esgrima de Mar del Plata, Boca Juniors, Chacarita, Everton (in Chile), Deportivo Tachira (Venezuela) and Real Castilla. Hoyos and Messi immediately get on well. They talk about football and, of course, Leo's passion for Newell's. They very quickly understand each other. The new coach's first impression occurs on Japanese soil at the beginning of August 2003, where the youth B team is about to compete in the Toyota International Youth Under 17 Football Championship. 'When I arrived,' says Hoyos, 'we did some light training to loosen up. Nothing particularly hard or revealing. But after five minutes I could hardly believe it. Of course, they had told me about him. But I didn't realise the extent of it: Leo was fierce.'

A thought that is reinforced during the first match against Feyenoord in Aichi. Fifteen minutes after kick-off, Barça are already down by a goal. Leo calls for the ball, dodges past four defenders and the goalkeeper, and gifts Songo'o a goal. Hoyos cannot believe his eyes: on the one hand he is surprised by the boy's generosity, not at all selfish like so many others his age (or older); on the other hand he is dazzled by his class.

Leo goes on to be chosen as player of the tournament. It is a title he will receive again at the XXIII Torneig de Futbol Formatiu Memorial Jaume Serra in Sitges, at the third Memorial Salvador Rivas Miró in Sant Vicenç de Montalt, and at the Torneo dell'Amicizia, which is played at the end of August in San Giorgio della Richinvelda, in the Italian province of Pordenone. The youth B team defeats Parma, as well as host region Friuli-Venezia-Giulia, Hansa Rostok, Eintrach Frankfurt and Treviso, and in the final they beat Juventus 4-0. The team racks up 35 goals in total, but Leo cannot forgive himself for having missed a penalty. Although the wound is somewhat healed by converting one in the final, the error still haunts him. At first, Hoyos tries to console him by saying the goalkeeper will be able to tell his children and grandchildren that he once saved a penalty taken by the greatest player in the world; then he sets him to work training daily from the penalty spot, explaining that over the course of a season he will have to shoot five or six times from there and any one of those could be decisive. It could be in a championship game or in an important tournament. They are words that will come back to Leo when Argentina win the Under 20 World Cup thanks to two of his penalties.

Nonetheless, the Hoyos/Messi winning partnership (only a single defeat, at the hands of Real Madrid in the José Luis Ruiz Casado Sant memorial tournament) does not last long – only for the pre-season. The club's directors are in no doubt: Leo is outgrowing this particular league. They decide to move him up, along with Gerard Piqué, to the youth A team.

It is here that the youngster's incredible rise begins. In just one season he moves from the youth B to A team, then up through the Barcelona ranks from Barça C in the

Third League to Barça B in the Second B League, not forgetting his brief moment of glory with the first team as well as reappearances in the youth leagues to help out his ex-team-mates. Here is a more detailed account of Messi's performance and shining moments during his time with each of those three teams.

The youth A team – he arrives on the third match day of the league. He stays until Christmas, although for a few weeks he also plays for the Barça C team, returning at the end of May for the Copa del Rey. He plays in eleven championship matches and scores eighteen goals, one of which is truly incredible. It is against Real Betis during the final of the Nerja tournament. Messi finds himself in the centre of the pitch and, seeing that the goalkeeper has moved much too far forward off his line, shoots hard. The ball flies in a perfect arc: goal and victory.

Barça C team – at the end of November 2003, things are going badly for the team, who have only managed nine points in fourteen games. Enter the reinforcements: Messi and Alfi from the youth A team. They win their first match on 29 November against Europa. The two of them play extremely well. But the best moment comes on 4 January 2004. They are playing against Gramenet in Santa Coloma. The Blaugrana are losing 2-1. In the 87th minute it is Leo's turn to shine. A header and a left-footer – bim bam boom – two goals in the blink of an eye (in addition to the equaliser), and the Flea brings home the victory for his team. Five goals in ten games, a determining factor in helping to get out of the relegation zone, and Leo moves on to better things. He is too good for the Third League, it would be better to try him in a higher league, despite the fact that he is only sixteen years old.

Barça B team – on 16 March, he plays his first match at home against Mataró. Coach Pere Gratacós admits that they had to create a special training programme just for him, as he would have to face older boys who were taller, stronger and more experienced. The coach also confesses his astonishment at the way in which the youngster was able to switch teams, team-mates, coaches and formations, and yet still give it his all. He plays five matches and only the first is a victory – but Gratacós says that he was acclimatising and eventually showed what he could do. He adapted to the league and in the match against Girona he was the best on the field, which, like snakes and ladders, takes us back to square one: the youth B team. 'Others would have got annoyed, but not him,' says Juan Carlos Pérez Rojo, his youth team coach. 'When the youth B team needed him, he immediately said yes.'

It happens in the last three games of the 2003–04 Liga. Three teams are still in the running for the title: Espanyol, Barça and Premià de Mar. The decisive encounter with Espanyol is on 15 April. If the parakeets pull it off they will be one step away from the title. By contrast, Barça cannot afford to put a foot wrong if they want to keep their options open until the end. So Leo pulls a majestic game out of his hat, and when the opposition, losing 2-1, start looking dangerous while desperately chasing the draw, Messi responds in his own way – with a goal that seals the deal.

Two weeks later, the team is celebrating, having won the title. His 36 goals in official matches, and 50 counting friendlies, are worth a considerable amount, not to mention his first professional contract. The negotiations are not easy given the many differences between the club's directors and Jorge Messi, who deals with the matter personally. Eventually, however, a deal is reached. The Barça bosses know that should Leo decide to leave the city, he would have other options. Cesc Fàbregas has already been lost to Arsenal during the confusion that followed the dismissal of Joan Gaspart. They do not want history to repeat itself.

Chapter 14

Home-grown

Conversation with Cristina Cubero, Mundo Deportivo (Sports World) *journalist*

What does Leo Messi represent for Barça?
'For Barcelona – and for the world – he represents the wait for a player like Maradona. A player who can enter the halls of fame among the footballing greats: Pelé, Maradona, Cruyff.'

Is he a player who responds to the club's values?
'Yes, definitely. I think they are "more than just a club" to him. The way they signed him – he had a growth problem but they made a huge push for him. It's about more than just football. And another thing – Barcelona has always favoured players who are talented and technically skilled, and he is one of them. And what's more, Messi is a kid who has grown up through the Barça ranks, among us. He is one of us, he is home-grown. He has grown up in the Blaugrana culture. And the Barcelona locals really appreciate that. Let's not forget that there is a tradition around here of going to see the youth teams play. Many people knew who Leo was from the youth leagues and they know what it takes to get to the first team. That's another reason to love him.'

When did you first meet Messi?

'I have known him since he was sixteen years old. I've followed his whole career, both at Barça and with the Argentine
national team. I still remember the first time I interviewed
him ... He was a shy kid, but he surprised me when he said he
didn't enjoy watching football ... he liked playing it. Or that
time in Hungary, when he cried all night because he had
been sent off during his first game with the Albiceleste.'

How has he changed over the past few years?

'In terms of football I think things have fallen into place
for him since those goals against Getafe and Espanyol. He's
no longer a clone of Maradona, he is his own person now,
he's Leo Messi. He has had lots of opportunities to put into
practice all the skills that he has stored away; he absorbed
it all from Diego, all those images that he's seen thousands
of times. He's shown that he knows how to do it. That's it.
Now he can develop his own personality. He's not the kid
who cries any more, or who stamps his feet like he did in
the Champions League final in Paris, when he didn't get a
medal – he's matured. If he gets angry, he says so, he shows
it openly, like when he dedicated his goals to Ronaldinho.
And his social scene has changed a lot. I think he has come
to realise what he represents, and the atmosphere that he
generates, especially after last year at the Copa América in
Venezuela, when an entire stadium was screaming his name.
It must have been a shock, something that is not easy to get
used to. But the good thing is that the fame hasn't gone to
his head. He behaves the same way as he did before, despite
having no privacy. A good example of that happened a few
months ago in Rosario when a kid stopped him at a traffic
light. He wants a photo. The normal thing to do would be for
Leo to wind down the window and let him take a photo on
his phone. But no. Leo parks and gets out for a picture.'

Has his role in the dressing room changed?
'He's not the captain, but in terms of football he's a sporting leader, and no one disputes it. His team-mates know exactly what they can expect from him, and everyone knows how valuable he is.'

Once Joan Laporta arrived Ronaldinho became Barcelona's icon, now it is Messi. What are the differences between them?
'Ronaldinho was a trickster, an artist with the ball. Leo represents the essence of the game: speed plus skill.'

Chapter 15

Videotape

29 June 2004

Hugo Tocalli tells the following tale: 'They brought me a videotape of a boy who was playing in Barcelona. I really liked what he could do, but ... in those sorts of cases I'm always worried that the tape is from some footballing agent. Besides, the kid was very young ... So I said to myself, no ... I'll wait a while. I go off to Finland with the Under 17s and when I get back I find out more about this player. Everyone has told me great things about him. I go and see Grondona (Julio Grondona, the president of the AFA – the Argentine Football Association), and I schedule an opportunity to see the kid, in two friendlies, against Paraguay and Uruguay.'

The kid was Leo Messi, an unknown from the other side of the Atlantic. And the famous tape that was sent to Tocalli (who was then responsible for the Federación Argentina youth division, and is now the coach at Colo-Colo, a Chilean first-division club), came from Claudio Vivas, assistant to Marcelo 'el Loco' ('Crazy') Bielsa, who at the time was manager of the Argentine national team, and today is the Chilean national coach. Vivas, at that time an ex-Newell's player and coach, had been curious about this fellow Rosarino, an ex-leper like himself, whom he had met many years previously at the Escuela de Fútbol Malvinas, and who was now making waves in Europe. So curious, in fact, that he decided to submit a tape of some of his fellow countryman's best moments for the coach's judgement.

It works, and the two proposed friendlies are subsequently organised in order to see him in action. The first request sent to Barcelona at the beginning of May has his name spelt incorrectly, asking for them to spare 'Leonel Mecci' some time to come over to Argentina; the request is politely rejected. He has Copa del Rey commitments. The end of June is more suitable. The AFA are in a hurry to see him play. Leo has lived in Spain for three years, he plays in the Barça youth leagues, and there is a risk of losing him and seeing him in a *Furia Roja* (Red Fury – Spanish national) shirt. It is not such a remote possibility given that only a year earlier during the Copa de España in Albacete, Under 16 coach Ginés Menéndez had offered Leo the chance to play for Spain. 'No thank you' was the reply he received. Despite living on the Iberian peninsula, Leo feels deeply Argentine. But who knows, perhaps after some insistence, the kid might change his mind? Either way, it is better to pre-empt the Spanish Football Federation.

'He arrived one Monday to train with the Under 20s,' recalls Tocalli. 'He was a very shy kid, he didn't know anyone and no one knew him.' While his team-mates – the likes of Pablo Zabaleta, Oscar Ustari, Ezequiel Garay – had already made names for themselves in the local championship, he has not. He stays in a corner of the dressing room at the Argentino Juniors stadium, hardly uttering a word. When the moment arrives to train and play ball, his attitude changes. Suddenly he is not as timid as perhaps he first seemed. The boss likes him – he values his ability and speed, but he does not come across too strong.

The match against Paraguay is on 29 June. Leo is not starting, partly because of his age, partly out of respect to the team, and also because they do not want to put too much pressure on him. In the second half, in the 50th minute, when the Argentines are already winning 3-0, Tocálli approaches him. He puts a hand on his shoulder and says to him: 'Go with the trainer, who is heading down to the pitch.' Surprised and excited, the Flea bursts onto the pitch wearing the sky-blue-and-white shirt for the first time. And he shows what he can do: he picks off his opponents and scores a goal.

'You could see it in the way he played,' says Tocalli. 'If he was good in training, on the pitch he was something else.' The friendly ends 8-0 and the youngster has seriously impressed the coaches. So much so that, that very night, Tocalli receives a call from his friend and youth coach predecessor, José Pekerman. 'He asked me where I had found the boy. He thought he was fantastic. "You're going to start him in the next match against Uruguay, right?" he asked me.' But no. In the match against Uruguay, in Colonia, he is not in the starting line-up. When he comes on, however, he surprises everyone again. The next day, Sunday 4 July, the Buenos Aires sports magazine *Olé* writes: 'Young Messi is the real deal. He scored two goals, four assists, and was the one to watch in the 4-1 victory over Uruguay.'

Leo's double trial has been a definitive success. He has really impressed them. And now Tocalli has no doubts about including him in the squad for the FIFA Under 20 World Cup qualifiers in South America the following January.

A bit of trivia: aside from Mauro Andrés Zanotti who plays in Ternana, Italy, Messi is the only 'foreigner'; he is also the youngest in the group. While he has just turned seventeen, the others are aged between eighteen and 20 and have extensive experience at all levels of the Argentine championship.

And then the South American qualifiers come around. They are played in Colombia – in Armenia, Manizales and

Pereira, cities along the central southern Andes, in the so-called 'coffee-growing region', far from Bogotá, the capital. They are played at high altitude – from 1,650 metres in Armenia, to 2,500 in Manizales – and the Argentines do not find it particularly easy to acclimatise.

Messi debuts against Venezuela on 12 January 2005 at the Centenario de Armenia stadium. As usual, he is not in the starting line-up, but is on the bench. He comes on fifteen minutes after half-time to replace Ezequiel Lavezzi, who today is a tattoo-sporting Napoli centre forward. At that moment the Albiceleste are winning 1-0. Thanks to Leo, eight minutes later the scoreboard reads 2-0. The match finishes 3-0. The Venezuelan defeat is incontestable and Messi's contribution is significant. The scenario is repeated at the Palogrande stadium in Manizales, this time against Bolivia. At the beginning of the second half, the boss sends the number 18 on in place of Barrientos in order to form a more attacking line-up. 'And after five minutes, Messi showed everyone that he is first-class material,' writes the Argentine newspaper *Época*. 'He latched onto the ball halfway up the pitch, made an unstoppable run and crossed it into the back of the net. An excellent shot that must surely be in the running for the title of best goal of the entire Under 20 South American championship. And in the twelfth minute, Messi made it 3-0.'

Two days later comes the clash with Peru, and for the first time Messi is in the starting line-up. He will only start in three matches; for all the others Hugo Tocalli will put him on in the second half. Why? 'That was my decision,' says Tocalli, justifying himself. 'The boy still hadn't got into the rhythm of the entire team, he was used to playing in the Barça youth leagues, he didn't have the same intensity that's needed to play in South America ... they were very demanding matches. And to add to that his opponents were from the '85 leagues and two years make a big difference at that age. So I decided to use him with caution so as not to tire him out or give him too much responsibility.'

It is a choice that yields good results which are obvious by the last match, against Brazil in Manizales on 6 February. Messi comes on for Neri Cardoso in the 65th minute. Ten minutes later he makes the' most of a pass from Barrientos and seals a 2-1 victory with a smooth shot into the back of the net, his first goal against the eternal rivals. At the end of the run, Argentina qualifies in third place for the FIFA Under 20 World Cup in Holland, behind Colombia and Brazil. Messi has scored five goals – the second highest goal-scorer after the Colombian Hugo Rodallega, who netted eleven. Rodallega is a nineteen-year-old who makes no concessions, be it on the pitch or in stirring up rivalries: 'I'm undoubtedly better than Messi,' he declares, 'but the big difference is that he plays for Barcelona and I play for Quindío.' Leo responds with humility: 'I have nothing to say, I play for the team.' And FIFA rightfully counts him among the eleven best players in South America – an accolade that helps to win over the selector.

'I loved him,' confesses Tocalli. 'I loved his change of pace from zero to a hundred in no time at all, his trick of dodging past his opponent, his ability to move extremely fast with the ball still glued to his foot. He demonstrated that, despite his stature, he was able to score many goals; he had a very good left foot and he would strike the ball well.'

For Hugo Tocalli, however, the match against Brazil was his last as the Under 20s coach. Pekerman, who has just been named manager of the Argentine national team, wants him by his side as a full-time assistant in the run-up to the Germany World Cup. Francisco 'Pancho' Ferraro takes over the reins of the Under 20 team due to play in Holland in June. During the final four months in the lead-up to the trip to Europe, Pancho alters his team. In come Agüero – today a much sought-after striker for Atlético Madrid (who played back then for Independiente, an Argentine team) – and Gago (who was then at Boca Juniors and today plays for Real Madrid); out go Boselli and Zanotti. At the last minute he has to replace José Sousa, from Estudiantes de La Plata, who has fractured his left hand. Likewise, he ends up having to replace many other players, just as his predecessors have had to do, as those who are committed to starting with their various Argentine teams are unable to play. Messi becomes a key figure on the team: he has just won the league with Barcelona and everyone is expecting him to reach his full potential in Holland. One thing for sure is that the Argentine team is one of the favourites to win the tournament. They are going for their fifth title in this competition. They won three out of four times (in Qatar in 1995, in Malaysia in 1997 and in Argentina in 2001), all under Pekerman's reign, and let's not forget the 1979 victory in Japan, where Diego Maradona was the protagonist.

It is Saturday 11 June: they are playing the United States at the FC Twente stadium in Enschede. Surprise! Messi is not in the starting line-up, he is on the bench and the Albiceleste lose 1-0.

It's a bad start to the tournament but Leo keeps everybody calm: 'I'm in a very good state of mind and I think I'm up for playing for 90 minutes, but I have to respect the coach's decisions.' He adds: 'The team will pick up the pace because we have some good players. We have everything we need to qualify.' He is spot on and he proves it on 14 June against Egypt. This time he is in the starting line-up. He scores the first goal, weakening the African defence, leaving Zabaleta to seal the scoreline definitively. The third match against Germany is a tricky one: it decides who goes into the last sixteen. The Germans have one point more than the

Argentines, so a draw will suffice for them to go through. But Messi makes his mark. He gets the ball in the middle of the pitch, slaloms past the defenders and makes a precise pass – Oberman lets the ball go past him and Neri Cardoso scores to make it 1-0.

The path to the final is full of obstacles: the first is Colombia, the winning team in the South American playoffs. Messi is suffering from an absence of players able to pass to him; nonetheless, in the twelfth minute of the second half he manages to level the score, making up for the first goal scored by the 'coffee-growers'. The introduction of Gago, Pablo Vitti and Emiliano Arementeros brings fresh legs to the team and, in the 93rd minute, Julio Barroso manages to avoid extra time. Spain awaits them in the quarter-finals. It has been widely written about as a greatly anticipated match, because the Spaniards are the current European Champions and they reached the final of the last Under 20 World Cup, although Brazil clinched the title in the end. Speaking of duels, there are great expectations about seeing Messi and Cesc go head to head, two eighteen-year-olds (Leo's birthday was the day before the match), friends from Barcelona and rivals on the pitch.

'I've got on well with Messi ever since the first day we met in the youth academy. I've spent three amazing years with him, scoring goals and doing one-twos. I've had a great time with him, it was amazing to play alongside him,' says the 'Wonderkid' – as the Arsenal fans call Fàbregas.

'Cesc is a good friend of mine – we met back in the Barça youth leagues. He's an impressive, well-rounded player, with many attacking and defensive skills,' replies Messi. And he assures everyone that he and his team have great respect for Cesc and Llorente's Red Fury team. The game is actually very balanced at 1-1 until the 70th minute. Then Spain loses concentration and Leo cranks it up a notch: first he serves up the advantage goal on a silver platter to Gustavo Oberman, then two minutes later, after chipping the ball over the head of one of his opponents, he scores the 3-1 winner.

'The Argentine team is the rightful winner, they have played better than we have,' admits Iñaki Sáenz. Regarding Lionel, he comments: 'He is talented, he makes good decisions, he looks for the goalkeeper and he knows what to do.'

The semi-final is the moment for the classic Argentina-Brazil clash, both four-times champions in this tournament and the memories of all the previous duels weigh on their minds – like in Qatar in 1995, when the goals of Leonardo Biagini and Francisco Guerrero claimed victory for the Albiceleste. The Argentines are playing with black armbands as a symbol of mourning – after two weeks in a coma due to a road accident, Independiente goalkeeper and national Under 17 player Emiliano Molina has just died. Within eight minutes the Albiceleste are already dominating, thanks to a torpedo-like shot from Messi from outside the area, which just edges in at the goalpost, rendering the Brazilian goalie's spectacular dive completely futile. Renato equalises in the second half, but at the last minute, after Leo gets past his opponent for the umpteenth time, Zabaleta picks up a rebound off a Brazilian defender and manages to score. And then comes the final, at 8.00pm on 2 July at the Galgenwaard Stadium in Utrecht. The opposition are Nigeria, who have beaten Morocco in the semi-finals. The previous day, a Dutch TV channel had presented Messi with a golden clog, the trophy that declares him player of the tournament. 'I'm very happy and I thank you for this prize,' he says. 'The truth is that I'm very surprised at everything that has happened to me here.' And the surprises continue into the final. In the 38th minute, Messi controls the ball

down the left-hand touchline; he begins a 45-yard zigzag-
ging run and gets into the box. Dele Adeleye realises that
he cannot snatch the ball from him and instead knocks him
down. There is no doubt in referee Terje Hauge's mind:
it's a penalty. Leo takes it without a run up, softly, with his
left foot, to the right of Vanzekin – who throws himself in
exactly the opposite direction: 1-0. In the 52nd minute
Chinedu Ogbuke levels the scoreboard for Nigeria. In the
73rd minute Agüero is fouled by Monday James in front of
goal. Leo steps up to the spot once more and shoots with
precision into the left-hand side of the goal. Goooaaaal: 2-1.
The Argentines win their fifth Under 20 title. Leo Messi is
the star player.

'What can we say about him? The final images of last
night sum it up,' writes *Clarín* the next day, 'with the trophies for best player and highest goal-scorer of the tournament, the champion's medal around his neck and the
sky-blue-and-white flag over his shoulders.'

Chapter 16

The football is his toy

Conversation with Francisco 'Pancho' Ferraro

With an air of intelligence in the dugout and a soothing, calming voice, Pancho – as he is known to everyone in the footballing world – has an enviable CV, between national youth teams, and clubs in both South America and Europe. But some of his best memories are still of those days in June and July 2005, when he led the Under 20s to their fifth world title.

'It's true, I am proud of that victory on both a personal level and as part of the team, I'm proud of what the boys did, and of players like Messi, Agüero and Gago, who made a name for themselves at international level.'

Do you remember the first time you saw Messi?
'Yes, it was in the South American qualifiers in January 2005, I was lucky enough to spend almost 40 days with the team. José Pekerman had asked me to take over the Under 20s and Hugo (Tocalli, the coach) wanted me to be there alongside him in Colombia to see how things were run.'

What was your first impression?
'That of a nice, polite, shy boy. He was the youngest of the group. He came from Europe and he still wasn't fully integrated, and he didn't have the physical stamina to play 90 minutes. That's why, after discussing it with Hugo, we

always brought him on in the second half, where he could make a difference.'

You didn't bring him on in the first game in Holland against the United States either ...
'He had a slight injury, which is why he was on the bench, but from the second match against Egypt he was in the starting line-up, and indisputably so. He had come better armed both physically and mentally from Barcelona. He had debuted with the first team, he was stronger and he knew how to handle a higher-level match. He played as an attacking midfielder, not as a playmaker; from three-quarters of the way up the pitch he could create risky situations at any moment. His presence on the team made all the difference.'

And how did he get on with the group?
'He was happy, and even happier when he was on the pitch with the ball. He shared a room with Agüero and he never bothered us. On the contrary, we could all see that they were happy and they got on very well. They were very considerate to their peers and to the staff. Very respectful. They brought sobriety to the group and kept low profiles – they were very humble. In fact, within a team full of honest people, they were two extremely respectful and professional boys.'

You say that Messi was always happy when he was on the pitch with the ball ...
'Yes, it bears repeating that Leo loves to play, and the football is his favourite toy; he has so much fun with it and he can control it like nobody else. It's incredible to see him on the pitch with the ball glued to his left foot; he drives it forward at a dizzying speed and he's aware of everything that

is going on around him; he reads and anticipates the play. That's very difficult – only the greats can do that.'

Like Maradona?

'Diego was one of a kind. It's true that for some time now everyone has been comparing the two of them, especially after Leo's goal against Getafe. All I can say is that both have truly been bewitched by a magic wand. But Messi doesn't need to be compared to anyone, he is a brilliant and unique footballer, a great one, one who can create surprises in every game and that is what people love about him.'

What did that Under 20 World Cup mean to Messi?

'It was his explosive moment as a footballer. It was his chance to make himself known across half the world. Before he went to Holland, very few people in Argentina knew of his talents; when he returned he was an idol. Best player, highest scorer of the tournament, those two goals of his in the final ... He was already a star, the footballer that an entire nation had been waiting for.'

And an entire nation was hoping that he would play in the 2006 World Cup against Germany. But Messi stayed on the bench. You were at the World Cup with the kids who were sparring with the team; you've known José Pekerman for years – what happened in that final match?

'We were down one substitution due to Pato's [Abbondanzieri's] injury and at that moment José will have decided to go for some other play, a different footballer, a different tactical move. But I have no doubt that Pekerman has been one of the best youth coaches. Who else could have brought the best out of an eighteen-year-old boy like Messi?'

Let's leave polemics to one side and talk about his development after that World Cup.

'I think Messi keeps on progressing and for the moment he has no limits. He progresses while keeping the same low profile as always. He doesn't like being evaluated, he doesn't do things just for the sake of doing them, he just wants to play in peace. He surrounds himself with his loved ones, his parents and his siblings, and they support and protect him, just as they did in Holland during the World Cup.'

Chapter 17
A friend

Conversation with Pablo Zabaleta

'He's a very good person,' says Leo's mother Celia, of Pablo Zabaleta. And she is happy that her son is near the Under 20s captain who won the World Cup, was later a winger with RCD Espanyol, and is now at Manchester City. He grew up in Arrecifes, and before making the move to Europe he cut his teeth at San Lorenzo (Argentina). And although he is only 25, everyone already considers him a veteran, or in other words, someone you can trust.

When did you meet Leo?
'In the Under 20 team when we won the Holland World Cup, which was an amazing experience and a joyful moment for all of us. That's where the beautiful friendship was born. We also became close with Kun (Agüero) and Oscar (Ustari). That was a great team ...'

What was so special about it?
'There was a good atmosphere, great camaraderie, and everyone really wanted to win ...'

But Leo didn't find it easy to integrate ...
'No, I don't think he did ... The problem was that no one knew him. He had come here very young, to Spain, and he had taken a different path. In Argentina, the players move

up to the first teams very young and that makes them grow up faster, it makes them find the right rhythm. Leo came from Barcelona, but it didn't take him that long to adapt and by Holland he really took off. The world went crazy for the way he played.'

And after that World Cup there were many more important moments.
'In Budapest I shared a room with him on the day of his debut with the national first team, although it wasn't a great game for Leo. A happy moment that we shared was winning the Olympic gold in Beijing.'

And what is your relationship like, now that you live in Manchester?
'We speak a lot on the phone and we see each other when the national team meets. Before, when I lived in Barcelona, we used to go out to an Argentine restaurant. Our favourite dish? A good rump steak. On other occasions we'd meet up in the afternoon to drink *mate* and talk football – the Argentine league, the national team, and whatever was happening in Spain.'

What is Messi like from a friend's point of view?
'He's a pretty normal guy. He's someone who likes to be at home and who loves his family very much. I think he's an even better person than he is a footballer.'

And what is he like as a footballer?
'As a player he's a gem. He has the heavenly gift of handling the ball really well. He impresses me with his ability to move the ball at such speed. It's incredible, what he's capable of doing, the way he gets round the other players, the way the ball is always glued to his foot. As he has shown

us many times, he's capable of taking a team to greater heights, of deciding a match. And he doesn't feel the pressure. Unbelievable. Leo is similar to Maradona, although Diego is unique and to compare them is crazy. As a friend I'm happy that he is doing so well.'

So, what did you mean when you said that 'he's an even better person than he is a footballer'?
'I said that out of humility towards Leo. He hasn't changed since I've known him. Fame hasn't made him lose himself, the praise hasn't gone to his head. He is still a great friend.'

Chapter 18
Soap opera

3 October 2005

The 2005–06 Liga begins on 26 August. The 75th Liga season has a new protagonist in the form of Robinho, the jewel in Real Madrid's crown, who it is hoped will sparkle alongside the other Brazilians in the league, Ronaldinho and Ronaldo. It is a league marked out as always by an eternal Real Madrid-Barcelona duel. The reigning champions play the first match away, against Alavés at the Mendizorroza stadium. Messi is neither on the pitch nor on the bench. Strange, given that only two days previously the young Argentine was the indisputable star of the Gamper Trophy. The explanation is given via an official announcement:

'FC Barcelona has decided not to play Leo Messi in the match against Alavés as a matter of caution, in light of the outstanding legal issue that will shortly be resolved within the confines of federal regulation relating to non-EU players.'

What has happened? On 8 July the Spanish Football Federation modified its general regulations regarding 'naturalised' players: in other words, non-EU players between the ages of seventeen and nineteen who have moved up through the youth teams of a Spanish club. The modification should allow the young player in question to play in the league, even if by doing so their club exceeds the three-foreigners-per-club limit in their line-up. Messi meets all of the required criteria to fulfil this regulation, which means that despite the club's three non-EU positions already being filled by Ronaldinho, Eto'o and Márquez, he should be able to play. But the new ruling – criticised by certain clubs, who see it as an ad hoc measure for Barcelona and Leo – must first be accepted by the Professional Football League (PFL) and ratified by the Consejo Superior de Deportes – the High Sports Council. In other words, 'due to the temporary situation, the FC Barcelona legal department have advised against allowing him to play'.

It is a difficult scenario to comprehend, given that in the 2004–05 season Leo played in a Champions League game with the first team against Shakhtar Donetsk, as well as in seven league games – with no professional licence and no EU documents, only his contracts for the youth team and the Barcelona Second Division B team. He had debuted in the Catalan derby against RCD Espanyol on Saturday 16 October 2004 in the Olympic stadium in Montjuïc. He comes onto the pitch to replace Deco and gets his first touch ten minutes later, after a pass from Belletti: some interesting action, but nothing exceptional that merits recording. Nonetheless, it is an unforgettable night for Leo – the realisation of a childhood dream, just as he was quoted in *La Capital* as saying that his goal was to 'make it into the first team'. Although, at that time, he thought he would do it at Newell's, his favourite team.

And he not only gets his premiere, he also scores his first league goal. It is 1 May 2005, the Nou Camp scoreboard indicates that there are three minutes remaining, and Barça are 1-0 up against Albacete. Frank Rijkaard brings off Samuel Eto'o, substituting Messi into the unusual position of centre forward. The youngster, only seventeen years and ten months old, takes advantage of a ball from Ronaldinho and beats the keeper, Valbuena, with a smoothly-timed shot.

It is a moment of pure elation: Leo does not know what to do with himself, and ends up being hoisted onto his friend Ronnie's (Ronaldinho's) shoulders, screaming joyfully. He is the youngest player in the club's history to score in a league game (a record later broken on 20 October 2007, when Bojan Krkić scored against Villarreal).

Things have gone well for him in the first team, but after that 1 May match, the Argentine will not play another official match that season – not even after Barça have done enough to ensure their seventeenth league title.

At the start of the 2005–06 season, he does not even play in the Spanish Super Cup against Betis. In the first leg he is on the bench, in the return leg he is not even on the teamsheet. In fact, even before the official communication from the club, something is not right and the board knows it. Messi is an unresolved case. Criticisms begin pouring in to the club. Why wasn't this dealt with before? Why hasn't he been naturalised, given that Argentines can opt to take on dual nationality (Spanish-Argentine) after two years of residence in Spain?

With news of the possibility that Leo might not be able to play in the league come other suggestions, such as forfeiting him to another club who have a non-EU spot open. A suggestion that is immediately dismissed. The rumours about possible interest from other European clubs, like Inter, become more and more persistent. The Italian club's president, Massimo Moratti, has never tried to hide his interest in the player and has even made a financially attractive offer to Jorge Messi – who tries to use this bargaining chip to put pressure on Barcelona to resolve the issue.

Meanwhile, on 31 August (the closing date for new team signings), FC Barcelona renew Messi's licence as a youth player naturalised in the team that plays in the Second Division B. And on 16 September, the news that the player has signed a professional contract goes public. It will last for nine years, until 2014. According to various sources, his fees will increase to 3 million euros per season and the buyout clause to 150 million euros.

In reality, the announcement about the contract had already been made in June. 'A week after his eighteenth birthday, Leo Messi has received his greatest present. Team secretary Txiki Begiristain has travelled to Utrecht, Holland, with the player's father, in order to draw up his new contract, which guarantees him a place at the club until 2010,' reads the Barça website on 30 June, while the youngster is playing in the FIFA Under 20 World Cup.

There are various theories about this discrepancy over dates: some maintain that Messi, now legally an adult, simply accepted the new deal; others reckon that the contract was ultimately modified in September, because the player's father was not satisfied with some of the clauses about incentives; there are those who think that the length of the contract was increased, from the usual five years to the final nine; still others believe that the September agreement was nothing more than a declaration of intent, implying that a professional contact would be signed in accordance with all regulations the following year. The fact remains that the issue of the contract adds new material to the ongoing soap opera, which takes a new twist on 20 September. An overwhelming majority of the PFL committee votes against: the rule proposed by the Spanish Football Federation and the Association of Spanish Footballers concerning naturalised players will not come into effect. Those who are firmly in agreement with the Blaugrana president talk of a conspiracy against Barça, hatched by the powers that be in Spanish football. One sure thing is that Messi cannot play in the league. He *can* play in the Champions League, however, without any problem. After examining the documents sent

over by Barcelona, UEFA has agreed that he can play. They
recognise his naturalised status. There is nothing extraordinary about it – Leo has already played many games in the
European competition the previous season. And in the first
Champions League match, against Werder Bremen, the
most dangerous Group C opponent, the Argentine shines.
He comes on in the second half. He wins a penalty, which is
converted by Ronaldinho, and which puts paid to the hopes
of the Germans. It is an important moment, which can
only point towards him being placed in the starting line-
up for the next match, against Udinese at the Nou Camp.
But on the following day, 26 September, news arrives that
puts an end to previous issues. At 1.00pm, Lionel Andrés
Messi Cuccittini appears before Fernando Alberti Vecino,
the judge presiding over the civil register, and proclaims
'that he does not renounce his Argentine nationality; that
he swears allegiance to the King and obedience to the
Constitution and Spanish laws; that he chooses Catalan civil
residency; and that he petitions for the right to be inscribed
into the Spanish civil register'.

In short, Leo has secured Spanish nationality: he is now a
citizen of the EU. Barça presents the documentation to the
Spanish Federation. The response is immediate and positive: 'In accordance with the rule in force [the Federation]
recognises the aforementioned footballer's right to play
with his club, taking into account his Spanish status, which
is valid for any purpose.'

On 1 October, the sixth match day of the league, Leo
will be able to join his team on the pitch against Zaragoza,
with a weight lifted from his mind. That Saturday the Nou
Camp crowd treat him as if he is the saviour of the country.
Barça is losing 2-0. Leo comes on in the second half but does
not produce any miracles, although in the final moments

Rijkaard's team manages to pull off an extraordinary draw. All should be well that ends well – but not this time.

Two days later, on Monday 3 October, Deportivo de La Coruña – Barça's next opponents – send a letter to the PFL, copied to the Spanish Football Federation Competition Committee, in which they petition for an injunction, requesting an investigation into the Barcelona player's naturalisation case. 'The player's national licence,' write Deportivo, 'has been obtained (and therefore given) outside the usual period for obtaining licences, which ended on 31 August and will not open again until December.' The crux of the demand 'is the reestablishment of equality in the competition, which it is believed has been violated, although of course once the inquiry has been carried out, this matter of undue infraction of the rules will come to an end'. The Alavés bosses, who had already threatened to kick up a fuss, go even further: they petition the Professional League to ban Messi from playing. From their point of view, his licence to play is null and void 'in the eyes of the law, given that processing it implies an evasion of the law'. Why? Because 'Barcelona could not arrange Messi's professional licence before 31 August, the date when the window for such licences closes, since at that point he was still a foreigner,' explains Javier Tebas, who is not only the legal advisor for Alavés, but also vice president of the PFL. 'Now they have given him Spanish nationality and have obtained a youth licence for him, with the intention of backdating it to 31 August and with the hope of playing him, despite the fact that the window for new signings is closed.'

In other words, Leo cannot rely on his EU residency until January. Moreover, 'given the contract that has been signed, how can Messi play with his youth team licence for the first team?' asks Tebas.

Joan Laporta loses his patience, declaring: 'We have sufficient legal basis for playing him. I don't know what else they want from us. We tried to do everything by the book and now that he has a Spanish passport they keep creating problems. I don't know why everyone is taking such an interest in damaging the player's career. They are stirring up trouble to prevent Messi from playing with Barça.'

The Blaugrana president goes on the counter-attack, making historical references: 'I don't want to imagine the possibility that nowadays, in an era when democratic rights and liberties exist, we are going to drag up the past, like the Di Stéfano case.'

A few details to refresh the memory: Alfredo Di Stéfano, known as the Blond Arrow, arrived in Spain from Argentina in 1953 to play for Barcelona. But the intervention of people in high places ended up turning the matter into a national issue and invalidating the signing. Even the advisory board got involved in the matter, stating that, given the player's importance, he shouldn't be given an exclusively Catalan residency, and putting forward the 'fair' proposal that the footballer play alternating seasons for Barça and Real Madrid. Luckily for the Whites, it was a solution the Catalan club rejected.

But the past does not come back to haunt Barça. Laporta's concerns are only phantoms that do not reappear. One thing for sure is that the Messi case ends up all over the sports pages across the country and provokes a scandal in Argentina. The first ruling from the Spanish Football Federation's Competition Committee appears on 18 October, stating that 'due to his naturalisation, Messi can continue to play as a Spaniard'. This last is followed by outrage from Alavés and Deportivo, appeals and counter-appeals, rulings and fierce debates, but in the meantime, Leo keeps playing. With the exception of the match against

Deportivo, when Rijkaard decides to rest him because he has just returned from a match with the Argentine national team, and because the Galician team had threatened to contest the fixture if the Argentine was playing, the Blue and Claret number 19 continues his hard work in the league. The issue continues in dispatches until the following year, but does not really make itself felt on the pitch. And so the Flea debuts at the Santiago Bernabéu on 19 November. It is his first time playing in this classic derby. Less than a month later, on 14 December, he receives the Golden Boy award at the Nou Camp, the annual prize awarded by the Turin sports publication *Tuttosport* to the best Under 21 player. Thanks to his achievements in the Under 20 World Cup, Messi steamrollers his opponents: Wayne Rooney only scores 127 points against the Argentine's 225. It is another source of recognition, which comes at just the right time: the Germany World Cup is only six months away and all these honours transform the Flea into a more desirable entity in the eyes of both small and large sponsors.

From McDonald's to Pepsi, Spanish oil and gas company Repsol YPF to La Serenísima yoghurts, Lays crisps to Storkman shoes, Garbarino electrical appliances to MasterCard, dozens of them are bidding for Messi, who has just shared a set with Maradona. They are pictured together signing a television: 'Look at what they're signing, they're the best.'

Lionel plays with everyone and everything. 'Football: 30 pesos. Tennis ball: twelve pesos. A kilo of oranges – three pesos,' runs the MasterCard advert while showing clips of the youngster having fun with a football, a tennis ball and an orange, concluding: 'Discovering there's hope after Diego – priceless.'

He plays with sad children for Bubbaloo, he dances with the ball to a tango rhythm for Pepsi. And that's nothing compared to the latest campaigns, like the one with the Messiah who ascends to the heavens for A-Style, an Italian caps and sportswear brand, or the one where Messi appears disguised as a footballing grandma for an Air Europa advert at the end of 2007.

But there is no point wasting time describing images, it would be easier just to go to YouTube to see how advertisers have made use of the image and abilities of Messi the juggler to sell anything and everything.

By the end of 2005 and beginning of 2006, it is undeniable that in the public sphere Leo is considered a coveted trophy – as proven by the war sparked between American sports giant Nike and German triple-stripers Adidas.

Chapter 19
A breath of fresh air

Conversation with Fernando Solanas, Head of
Sports Marketing at Adidas Iberia

Is it true that Nike and Adidas, the giants of the sports store
world, ended up in court over Messi?
'It's true, but let me tell you the story from the beginning.
It was in 2003 that I first made contact with Jorge, Lionel's
father and agent. At that time Messi had a contract with
Nike, just for sportswear: in exchange for his image, they
supplied him with trainers, clothes, etc. Jorge told me that
they were happy with the American firm, who had made the
bid for him two years earlier when he was only fourteen and
played in the FC Barcelona youth team. It had not occurred
to him to change sponsor. But I did not want to lose the
contact and the following year (when Nike's sportswear
contract was ending) I spoke to him again, making him see
that there was good profit to be made if he negotiated with
us.'

Let me see if I've got this right. In 2003 Messi was only sixteen
years old and already a multinational company like Adidas was
trying to 'steal' him from the competition ...
'It's our job to be on the lookout for the stars of the future.
That's why we go to the experts in every sector. I played
football. I love the sport and I might have a fairly good eye
for players, but when it comes to deciding where to invest,

I trust only the opinions of the coaches, the scouts, the "talent-hunters": in short, those who work alongside the youngsters. And five years ago all of them were saying that Messi was the gem in the Barça youth squad. They predicted his explosion ... I couldn't waste any time.'

OK, let's continue with the story ...
'Once the Nike contract has ended, Jorge decides not to sign with anyone else. He keeps receiving sports products from Nike because they sponsor Barcelona, but he wants to wait before making a deal for his son. I see him play in the Under 20 World Cup in 2005, wearing Nike gear. Messi is already a first-team player at Barça and things go very well for him in Holland. At that moment I think some very interesting offers start to land on Messi's doorstep from other European clubs, like Juventus.'

And what happens in terms of sponsorship?
'Two days before leaving for Holland, Jorge signs a letter of intention with Nike. Then things get complicated: they negotiate for many months without reaching an agreement ... until we intervene. We make an interesting offer, both in terms of money and in terms of representing the Germany World Cup. And in January 2006 we sign a contract until June 2010.'

They say that in terms of money ... Adidas offered five times the annual income offered by Nike ... and we're talking more than a million dollars – true or false?
'The figures are always confidential, we can't reveal the conditions of the contract.'

*Alright, let's continue with the story because this is where the war
between Adidas and Nike begins. Why, when Messi first wore his
Adidas Predator outfit and scored a goal against Zaragoza in the
Copa del Rey did Nike scream at the top of their voices: 'Messi has
a deal with us and we're going to do whatever it takes for him to
honour it'?*

'Yes. Nike took the case to the courts and the judge cau-
tiously ruled that Leo had to play in Nike equipment, so as
not to hurt the supposed rights of the American firm.'

But in the end you won the battle, correct?

'I wouldn't call it a battle, but yes, the latest ruling was the
one that determined Messi had no obligations towards Nike.
Since then we have gradually started working with Leo.'

*What does Leo represent to the football world and to sports
marketing?*

'Leo is something new, a breath of fresh air, the new
Maradona. On the pitch it is like he is animated. In short, a
very attractive personality.'

*No one disputes his appeal on a footballing level, but as a
personality … isn't he a very shy and modest kid?*

'That's exactly what people like about him, that he's normal,
he's a kid who loves being with his family and friends, who
plays PlayStation and doesn't notice the buzz he generates.
His simple nature is his greatest advantage. Too often sports
stars seem to inhabit their own universe, very far from us.
Leo, with his shyness, is close to all the fans.'

*Let's talk about your campaign, 'Impossible is Nothing', in which
Messi is one of the key figures.*

'They are real stories that our icons tell. The idea is to con-
vey to the consumer that nothing is impossible. And in this

case Leo tells his life story: an eleven-year-old boy who had the physical stature of an eight-year-old, but who didn't let that stand in the way of succeeding. Through hard work, perseverance, willpower, nothing is impossible. Leo is a perfect example. It is worth remembering that at thirteen he crossed an ocean, arrived at Barcelona, and after starting in the youth teams he has made it as a global football star.'

On the topic of stars, let's compare: David Beckham versus Messi, or if you prefer, Ronaldinho, who's a Nike man, and Leo.
'They are different products. Beckham is 34. He has already reached his peak, he has had, and still has, an impressive public image in Europe, in Asia, in the United States – he's the pop star of football. Ronaldinho, on top of his smile, has already won everything. Leo still hasn't reached that level. But in any case, for us, since the 2006 World Cup, he has been a global icon alongside Beckham and Kaká.'

What does Leo sell?
'Authenticity.'

Where does he sell?
'He is strongest in Latin America, Spain and Asia, especially in Japan.'

Why Japan?
'Because Leo is small. It sounds silly, but it isn't. The Japanese identify with a little player who is skilled with the ball.'

How are things going in Europe?
'His image is growing. He has a lot of clout – in England, for example, thanks to the Champions League matches against Chelsea and Manchester United.'

And what does Adidas expect from Leo Messi in the future?
'That he continues making progress the way he has up until now. I think he is still a diamond in the rough. He still hasn't shown the extent of his brilliance.'

Aren't you worried that he will burn out, that media overexposure and publicity could damage such a young footballer, as has happened in many other cases?
'We will have to take good care of him and treat him well.'

Chapter 20

Boy of the match

22 February 2006

It is cold in London – intensely cold. The first leg of the Champions League quarter-final is being played at Stamford Bridge. The ground is muddy, which has provoked no end of controversy in the press. The atmosphere is heated – very heated, and very English. On one side is Chelsea – with a rational game, defensive, vigorous and impetuous, the most convincing team in Europe. On the other, Barça – talented, imaginative, with a taste for the spectacular. A lovely footballing model, but one that is often considered fragile, a machine easily broken. Both sides lead their respective leagues and, by the end of 2005, they have done incredible things. The new year has not started too well, however: in the Premier League, Chelsea let in three goals at Middlesbrough and they suffered the unspeakable in the FA Cup against modest Colchester. Barça are without Eto'o, who is playing in the African Nations Cup. With Xavi injured they have been knocked out of the Copa del Rey at the hands of Zaragoza, and without Ronaldinho they have lost two league games. The defeat against Valencia is tough, since they are closing in on Barça in the table, reducing the gap to six points.

Leaving circumstances to one side, the match offers myriad points of interest. Like the duels: between Ballon d'Or winner Ronaldinho and the runner-up Frank

Lampard; between Eto'o and Drogba, voted best and second best African players. And let's not forget the duel between the coaches: on the one hand emotional, hysterical José Mourinho and on the other, cool, calm Rijkaard: two completely opposing characters.

Moreover there is the eternal theme of revenge, or vengeance, which is always present in football. Few have forgotten the defeat and the three goals in nineteen minutes that the Blues had inflicted on the Blaugrana on 8 March 2005 in the return leg of the Champions League last sixteen. Barça led with a relative advantage after their 2-1 victory at the Nou Camp, but were left helplessly chasing the comeback after a series of defensive errors, which, according to Rijkaard, were due to a lack of maturity and concentration. Despite Ronaldinho's exploits and a string of missed chances, this Barça team, who already thought of itself as the new Dream Team, had to deal with the sight of Mourinho running onto the pitch and blowing kisses to the fans, as well as the insults, the shoving and the violent brawl between the players and the security guards, which even implicated the Dutch coach. The journey home was bitter, as the errors were rehashed over and over and referee Pierluigi Collina was accused (by the Spanish press) of not having given various penalties, nor having seen Carvalho's foul on Valdés in what was eventually a 4-2 victory led by Terry. Accused, in other words, of having favoured Chelsea.

It is well known that in cases such as these, history matters. It triggers headlines on every sports page and almost creates the impression of a television drama entitled 'Revenge'; there is more and more tension felt among the players, who go onto the pitch now at 8.45pm. The team-sheets are announced: Chelsea are missing Drogba, who is replaced in the attack by Hernán Crespo, while Asier del Horno and Claude Makelele are confirmed at the back.

Meanwhile Thiago Motta joins Edmílson in the centre for Barça. Andrés Iniesta, who has been in the starting line-up for some time, is on the bench. Leo Messi is sporting the number 30 fluorescent yellow shirt. To many, he seems no bigger than a kid when he comes onto the pitch. How will he be able to deal with this kind of tension, which is difficult enough even for the big boys? It seems that he doesn't feel the pressure. Is it down to a youthful lack of inhibition? Or is he simply fearless? The answer comes in the third minute, when the first shot on target comes from the Argentine and Petr Cech saves it comfortably. Leo is definitely fearless. And he demonstrates it continuously in the coming minutes as he scurries into every available space like a little mouse. He runs up and down, stealing balls, passing accurately, working well with his team-mates, creating the first real chance and sowing the seeds of panic among the Chelsea defence. A nightmare for Del Horno, who leaves a stud-mark impression through his right sock in the 31st minute. No caution, and no protest whatsoever from the Flea. Play continues. But a scuffle leads to the Basque defender being sent off six minutes later, leaving Chelsea a man short. What happens? Messi controls the ball three-quarters of the way up the pitch, resists an extremely tough tackle, and battles shoulder to shoulder with Robben, who manages to steal his position and snatch the ball, but the little guy will not back down. He chases him to the edge of the pitch, trying to overpower him from one side or another. Finally, with an unexpected burst of energy, he seizes the ball near the corner flag. Robben is now in front of him – he succeeds in nutmegging him but no sooner has he done so than he is flattened by a blue locomotive.

'I saw the defender coming at me fast and deliberately, and I jumped out of the way ... That's why I didn't make it,' the Argentine later explains. The yellow shirt is knocked to the ground, along with Del Horno's blue one. Players gather around them, causing a commotion. Robben and Gudjohnsen start arguing with the linesman. Deco and Ronaldinho throw themselves at Del Horno. Puyol almost comes to blows with Robben. Motta and Edmílson try to calm the situation. Terry argues with Terje Hauge, the Norwegian referee, while Ronnie mutters something in his ear. Then comes the red card: Del Horno protests, Motta applauds, Makelele complains. The game recommences and Mourinho readjusts his team. He substitutes Joe Cole, sending on right back Geremi, and moving Ferreira into position to mark Messi. But nothing changes, neither the foul nor the recent beating has fazed the youngster, who continues to take centre stage; he doesn't let up, he pays no attention to the Blues' exasperation, and soldiers on with his fearless solo performance. He continually empowers the right flank of the pitch, creating juicy chances for Ronaldinho and Deco, although they fail to take advantage of them. Leo is too isolated – without the team behind him, he fails to make an impact. In the meantime, ten-man Chelsea are adhering strictly to their coach's instructions: 'Just get the 0-0 draw.' Now they have the perfect excuse to hang back and wait for an opportune moment to strike. The Blues are in complete control and it's not long before they make it count: spurred on by Drogba's entrance at the beginning of the second half, the English team takes the lead in the 58th minute. It is Motta who ends up sliding the ball into his own net while trying to clear a free kick by Lampard. Now they need to turn the game around. Once again it is Messi who is trying everything possible, motivating the rest of the team and ignoring the chants and whistles from the Stamford Bridge crowd at every turn. Fast, direct, he skips away, destroying the defence, shooting, making incredible passes – but nobody is there to receive them. He puts in a gentle shot from the edge of the area which grazes the goal-post to the left of the Chelsea goalkeeper. And he stands there as if stunned, with an ironic expression, thinking how he could have done better. He is the most determined, and finally the team gets behind him. In the 70th minute Terry turns the tables for Barça: Ronaldinho takes a free kick that beats Cech to level the score and Barcelona start to play some good football and create chances. And it's Messi again: he sends a golden opportunity to Larsson, who has come on for Motta. Three minutes later, Terry launches himself onto the Argentine in the area to prevent him from controlling the ball. Penalty? The referee ignores the incident. In the 79th minute Eto'o heads a great pass from Márquez into the net. They have done it.

Unbeaten until that moment at Stamford Bridge, after 49 matches (38 wins, eleven draws), José Mourinho must face up to the blow of his first defeat. And he doesn't digest it very well. He blames it on the referee and Leo: 'Am I disappointed with Del Horno's sending off? Did you see the match? Either way I'm cross with the authorities: write that if you want ... But what can we do? Ask for them to retract Del Horno's red card? Suspend Messi for his theatricals? Nothing will change the result ... Because let's be serious, Messi put on an act. Catalonia is a country of culture, you know it is. And I've been to the theatre many times and it's very high quality over there. And Messi has learnt from the best ...'

'Whoever says that Messi put on an act obviously didn't see what really happened,' says Eto'o. 'They were pounding on him from all directions,' insists Rijkaard. Leo simply says: 'I have a cut on my knee, one on my thigh and another on my foot. My whole body is bruised, but I'm not in pain because we won.' He adds: 'It has been an incredible game.'

Everyone else is in agreement, starting with his team-mates, who hug him as he leaves the field, while the fans who came to the match chant his name. The following day the descriptions are flowing – people are talking of 'dedication', 'genius', 'a footballing virtuoso', 'Barça's treasure', 'the birth of a great star', 'the best', 'the bravest', 'the best in the match'. In the context of his age and his nerve, his performance is compared to the likes of Pelé in the 1958 World Cup in Sweden, of Maradona in the Under 20 World Cup in 1979, of Cruyff against Benfica in 1969, of George Best. He is showered with praise, it is as if the boy has passed the test of maturity with flying colours and, with him, the entire team.

The return leg at the Nou Camp is on 7 March. In the 23rd minute Leo Messi is off, stealing the ball from Robben – but suddenly he puts his hand to his left knee and falls to the ground. 'In the play when I collided with Gallas, I had already felt the first stabs of pain, but I decided to keep going,' he would say later, 'and in the next play I realised that I couldn't go on.'

There has been no rough play, no knock, but Leo is lying on the ground. He grimaces with pain, his hands holding back his hair and covering his face to try to hide his fear. The crowd falls silent. His team-mates look at each other, downcast. He leaves the pitch, distraught. Rijkaard hugs him, emotional. It is a difficult moment for a player who was applauded by 90,000 Nou Camp spectators – not as a drama queen, but as the puppet master who had pulled the strings of the Stamford Bridge victory.

Muscular tear in the upper part of one of the right hamstrings – a four-centimetre tear. The Barcelona medics say that recovery will take four to six weeks. But luck is not on Leo's side. When the time comes for him to play again, more problems arise in the same area: he can still feel the scar. He was supposed to play against Villarreal but does not, he should be playing in the Champions League semi-final against Milan but is not. In the end he goes 79 days without football. And he watches the Champions League final from the stands.

There had been talk of the possibility of him playing for a short stint on this great occasion – Barça-Arsenal at the Stade de France, Paris – perhaps for a few minutes at the very least, but despite the seemingly healed injury, Rijkaard decides not to risk it. His team-mates go on to lift the cup for the second time in Barça's history. Sad and alone, Leo does not go down to the pitch to collect his medal.

Chapter 21
Supersonic aesthetic

Conversation with Santiago Segurola,
Marca *journalist*

'The essence of football is contained in the body of a little player,
an eighteen-year-old boy who could pass by unnoticed on any
given street. His name is Leo Messi and there is every reason to
believe that we are in the presence of an exceptional player, the
most brilliant to appear in recent years.' Those are the first lines
of your article the day after Chelsea-Barcelona. Why did Lionel
impress you so much?

'Because that performance contained all the elements that
fascinate spectators and encourage you to contemplate
the wonder that is football. Because it didn't seem like a
match for an eighteen-year-old boy who had spent very little time at the top. In that match, before Barça appeared,
Messi appeared – he was surprising, skilful, speedy, intelligent, and he showed great courage. It was a boy who made
the difference in that match. He amazed the crowds. His
performance was one of the greatest I have ever seen in my
life.'

And have you seen many players?
'I saw Maradona when he was at the height of his career, I
saw Raúl on his debut ... but none of the players that I've
seen play were as powerful or as brave.'

What was his most impressive attribute?

'Speed, without a doubt. Nowadays in football everyone wants to be fast, but speed leads to collisions. Messi amazes me in the way that he knows how to make so many decisions at such high speed without getting it wrong ... Perhaps he doesn't have the imagination of Ronaldinho or the other great Brazilians, perhaps he doesn't have the vision or the game plan of a Maradona, but he has a supersonic aesthetic.'

Any other qualities?

'He is the only player capable of winning a match from anywhere on the pitch. He proved that against Zaragoza. He was halfway up the pitch, with his back to the goal, and he ended up scoring. He has the most extraordinary turn I have ever seen, more electric than Maradona's. He can dodge, he can "one-two", and he can finish ... He is the product of a new global academy of youth team players. He represents an interesting model: his Argentine roots are continuously apparent and, at the same time, he belongs to a culture and a style of play that is profoundly "Barcelonan". He is an example of the magnificent work that Barcelona has done with its youth academy since the Bosman ruling.'

How has Messi changed since that match?

'He hasn't changed, he has just become more important. Now Messi is the footballing leader of Barça and he has to lead his national team as well. It's a shame that in the Germany World Cup he wasn't a key figure, rather he was a problem. He was considered not ready; there was a pointless debate over whether he should start; they didn't know how to make use of his amazing qualities. They gave the reins to Riquelme, who is without a doubt a good player, he can win you matches, but he can also lose you some fundamental ones, like the one against Germany. He didn't stand out.'

Looking into our crystal ball: what do the coming years hold?
'What concerns me is the possibility of Messi losing speed. What will happen when time erodes his tenacity and his velocity? I don't know ... Will he end up like Ronaldo, who became a specialist in having six good moments per match and a 20-metre sprint? It's difficult to predict and it's difficult to say what effect all the merchandising will have on him. Publicity has often been known to confuse players. It obliges them to be the best in the world at every possible second. And that's not possible. A great player has to know how to choose his moments.'

So in the end the real dangers are the advertising and becoming a diva?
'I think that these players aren't prepared for the extreme tension generated by the press, the critics, the success, the fame, the celebrity, the travelling, the commercial demands of the sponsors. These things can be distracting, they can let you get comfortable in your daily routine of match-playing. Yes, footballers need to know that it's like being hit by a truck and it's a hard knock to take. Much harder than a few kicks from Asier del Horno at Stamford Bridge.'

Chapter 22

Difficult, very difficult

Conversation with Asier del Horno

Defender, born 19 January 1981 in Barakaldo (Vizcaya). Height: 1.81m. Weight: 72 kilos. Debut: 9 September 2000, Deportivo-Athletic Bilbao 2-0. Sporting career: 1999–2005 at Athletic, 2005–06 at Chelsea, 2006–07 at Valencia, 2007–08 at Athletic, 2008–2010 at Valencia. Ten caps with the Spanish national team. Titles: one Premier League (2005–06), and FA Community Shield (2005). That's how his CV reads, but the ex-Chelsea left back has many more things to say.

What happened at the 2005–06 Champions League final sixteen Chelsea-Barcelona match at Stamford Bridge?
'It was a special match, given what had happened the previous year. The atmosphere was tense. Everyone could feel it. We were quietly confident. Mourinho had prepared us for every detail of the encounter, trying to block every possible Barça manoeuvre. In the midfield we had people like Makelele, Lampard and Essien, who protected the defence but Messi kept on getting through. I came face to face with him two or three times and I tried to stop him with all my skills and experience.'

Did Messi surprise you? Perhaps you weren't expecting to come face to face with a kid like that?
'In every match there's always one player, the one you least expect, who makes you suffer.'

In the 31st minute, you gave him a kick that merited a yellow card. What had the Argentine done to you?
'Nothing, it was an incident during the game and I don't remember the details.'

Is Messi one of those forwards who provokes the defence?
'No, he doesn't provoke. He doesn't say anything. There are many provocations in football between defenders and forwards, but that's not his style.'

Moving on to the 36th minute of the first half ...
'Messi had nutmegged Robben just by the corner flag. I tried to stop him and he went past me. He started to roll around on the ground and they sent me off. Messi was sharp, he was smart, it looked like it was an incredible tackle and in reality it was nothing ...'

So José Mourinho was right when he declared after the match that 'Leo Messi put on an act, and a good one'?
'Lionel exaggerated, without a doubt.'

Leaving the past aside, let's talk about Messi's characteristics as seen from the point of view of a left back.
'The key thing about Messi is that he drives the ball forward very well, quickly and with the ball always glued to his boot. His speed gives him time to change direction, surprising whoever is marking him at that particular moment.'

How can Messi be stopped?
'It's complicated. It's difficult, very difficult. Depending on the situation you're in, given his divine inspiration ... Playing on the opposite touchline, when he dodges into the centre, it's difficult to stop him. He has speed, he has skills ... argh, he's a real problem for any defender.'

Any advice for your colleagues?
'I wouldn't know ... I can only say that defenders need to keep tightly in line, be aggressive, be speedy and hold the position well.'

They say that Messi is now the best in the world – what do you think?
'I wouldn't venture an opinion about who is the best in the world. There are many great players: Cristiano Ronaldo, Kaká, Drogba, Villa.'

And Messi?
'Yeah, sure, he's among the best. He can make a difference, and he does spectacular things.'

And he drove you mad?
'Yes, but he's not the first ... How many times has Joaquín driven me crazy? That's just what happens to defenders ...'

Chapter 23

Not even a single minute

30 June 2006

There are others who are considered the big stars. Ronaldinho, more than anyone else; according to commentators and fans, he will be the one who will shine the most. Many predict he will be crowned best World Cup player and highest goal scorer. Because – among other reasons – according to the majority of the world's coaches, players, newspapers and TV channels, Brazil is favourite to take home the title. Betting on Barça's number 10 is easy and logical. He has just had a spectacular season: Ballon d'Or, Liga and Champions League winner. The only thing that remains in order to crown him king is his second world title. Here is the list of potential candidates: fellow Brazilian Ronaldo, from whom everyone expects the umpteenth resurrection; David Beckham, the pop star of football; Zidane – facing the final challenge of his career. They are closely followed by the likes of Figo, Ballack, Torres, Van Nistelrooy and Del Piero.

In terms of Argentina, the name on everyone's lips is Juan Román Riquelme. Twenty-eight years old, born in Buenos Aires, an attacking midfielder, he plays for Villarreal and as yet has no World Cup on his CV, but selector José Pekerman has put his trust in him.

The Albiceleste have been built around him and their game largely depends on Riquelme having a good day.

He is a silent footballer, charged with the responsibility of leading the team. He needs to be solid, he needs to play imaginatively and make magic, he needs to move between the lines and get the crucial passes to the strikers. And Messi? Well ... Messi is in the running in the category of medium-level stars, or rather, promising youngsters. He has been dubbed the new Maradona and the World Cup should be his chance to surprise the whole world at just eighteen years of age, after establishing himself on the international scene at Stamford Bridge.

Along with the Portuguese Cristiano Ronaldo and the Ecuadorian Luis Valencia, fans have included him in the list of six candidates from whom the best young World Cup player will be chosen (the other three, nominated by FIFA, are Cesc Fàbregas, the Swiss player Tranquillo Barnetta and the German Thomas Podolski). The title was inaugurated on 1 January 1985. The player in question will have to distinguish himself on pitches throughout Germany in terms of style, charisma, clean play and a passion for football. The Argentines want to see Messi in the starting line-up and they have pinned all their hopes on him; they want to see confirmation of all the amazing stories that are told across Europe about the heir to Maradona – and they want that confirmation in the shape of a national shirt. Since the days of the Pibe de Oro (Maradona's nickname) they have dreamt of a different player, a spectacular, magical player, whom they could love and worship the way they did – and still do – Diego. When it came down to it, it was Maradona himself who, a few months previously, asked that the number 10 shirt be given to Messi – a shirt number which the Argentine Federation had retired in his honour.

Leo may have grown up far from his native country, but in the last few months he has returned home in order to recover from the injury he received against Chelsea. He has had time to get some exposure, give interviews and shoot some ad hoc adverts for the World Cup. Both multinational and Argentine companies have bet on him in order to benefit from the effects of a global stage. Not least, German sporting brand Adidas, who have plastered entire buildings from Rome to Buenos Aires via Berlin with enormous posters of his face. On the eve of the World Cup, at least in terms of publicity, he is definitely beating his team-mates by miles. He undoubtedly has the highest level of media coverage of any Albiceleste player. But such publicity can generate jealousy – yet another obstacle in the youngster's path to being accepted in Pekerman's team.

He has recently been invited into the group, thanks to his success in the Under 20 World Cup. His debut with the main national team is on 17 August 2005. It is during a friendly against Hungary in Budapest, at the stadium dedicated to Ferenc Puskás. He comes on for Maxi López in the 65th minute. And he is on the pitch for little more than 40 seconds. On his second touch, he dribbles the ball past Vanczák. The Hungarian grabs him by his brand-new number 18 shirt; Messi lifts his arm and pushes him back. Bam! He catches the defender full in the face. German referee Markus Merk is in no doubt. He elbowed him. And he pulls out the red card in front of the disbelieving Argentines. Sent off in his first match. Not the scenario that Leo had imagined. He is to spend the rest of the match crying. His coach and team-mates think the referee's decision is excessive, but their words of consolation are in vain.

After an unfortunate debut, there are other matches that offer an opportunity to move on and get into sync with the squad. But it is not easy. As is already obvious, Messi is shy. He hardly speaks to his team-mates, or the staff. There is no shortage of anecdotes illustrating this, like the time during training in Madrid when the boss invites the whole squad to a barbecue – an Argentine social ritual *par excellence* – in order to encourage group bonding. Leo does not open his mouth, not even to ask for some meat. It is a silence that is apparent and worrying to the others. And Messi does not even emerge from his silence in order to conform to expected formalities. At Christmas, for example, when all the Argentine players go over to visit the manager after spending time with their families, Messi does not show up. And the AFA are often unable to locate him.

The lad adheres neither to the team hierarchy, nor to the unwritten rules that are essential to Argentine football. He is not a rebel, he does not behave badly, and he does not do it intentionally, it's just the way he is. In the training sessions before his debut with the main national team, for example, he finds himself face to face with Gabriel Heinze. He faces up to him one, two, three, four times, repeatedly giving him the cold shoulder. Heinze, now an Olympique de Marseille defender, is reaching boiling point and is about to avenge his wounded pride. Pekerman has to intervene to save the little guy's skin, and the honour of one of his players. It is a scene that will be repeated with others in Nüremberg, the Argentine team's base over in Germany. The least one could say about the young Barcelona footballer is that he is shameless. And without ignoring the issue of unwritten rules, which are steeped in history, it has to be said that Messi is young – too young. To draw parallels yet again, at eighteen years of age, despite being an emerging figure, Maradona was not even selected by César Bilardo for the 1978 World Cup. Messi is in Germany, but it should be remembered that no Argentine player since the 1930s has played in the final stages of the competition at only eighteen years old. The lesson that has had to be learned by men who have sat 'willingly' on the bench is that it is necessary to protect newly emerging talents at all costs – the weight of defeat must not be allowed to rest on their shoulders. There is actually a risk of harming them. And in these cases, history carries a lot of weight.

So too does the injury of 7 March. Messi is seemingly completely recovered; he has already played various friendlies before the World Cup; but there are those in the dressing room who say his muscles are still bothering him. In terms of his state of mind, he is happy in the lead-up to his first World Cup. In his pre-tournament statements he reaffirms what everyone has been saying: the Brazilians, with his friend Ronaldinho up ahead, are the favourites, but 'we also have a good team. And the national team is made up of many great players. Of course we are going to take it one step at a time, one game at a time. And there will be excellent opponents and every match will be very complicated. But I believe that Argentina can win the World Cup.'

The Albiceleste is in Group C, known from the beginning as the group of death: Ivory Coast, Serbia and Montenegro and Holland. It will not be an easy ride, especially with the disaster of the Korean and Japanese World Cup weighing on their minds.

Saturday 10 June at 9.00pm in Hamburg sees the first match against the Ivory Coast. During a training session five days earlier, Messi suffered a contusion, making it difficult for him to play. The manager's idea is to pace him, allowing him to go on later in the competition, apart from anything because they are not convinced he is 100 per cent fit. In fact, they state: 'We cannot promise anything that could create expectations. In each successive training session we have seen improvement and a return to form. And he is getting better bit by bit. We are grateful for the effort he has made to be here with us.' On the bench he goes. From his 'privileged' vantage point Lionel watches as Crespo scores his 30th Albiceleste goal with his usual opportunism. He watches as (*above*) Messi, front row, second from left, with his first team, Grandoli. The man in green is his father, Jorge Messi. (Courtesy of the Messi family)

(*below*) Celebrating with the trophy after Argentina beat Nigeria 2-1 during the 2005 World Championships Under 20 final. The banner in the background says: 'Argentina I love you'. (AP Photo/Bas Czerwinski)

(above) Tussling with Brazil and Manchester United's Anderson in the semi-final of the men's football competition at the Beijing Workers' Stadium during the 2008 Olympics. (PA Wire)

(below) Edwin van der Sar and Rio Ferdinand can only watch as Messi scores Barcelona's second goal in their 2-0 win over Manchester United in the 2009 UEFA Champions League final in Rome. (AP Photo/Gregorio Borgia, File)

(*above*) From left, Barcelona's Xavi Hernandez, Carles Puyol, Lionel Messi, Thierry Henry and Andrés Iniesta celebrate next to the trophy at the end of the 2009 UEFA Champions League Final against Manchester United. (AP Photo/Luca Bruno)

(*below*) Fighting for the ball against Real Madrid's Xabi Alonso, right, during a Spanish La Liga soccer match at the Nou Camp stadium in late 2009. (AP Photo/Manu Fernandez)

(above) Kissing his 2009 Ballon d'Or, or Golden Ball trophy, awarded to the Europe-based footballer of the year. (AP Photo/Francois Mori, File)

(below) Scoring the second and winning goal during the 2009 Club World Cup final against Estudiantes of Argentina in Abu Dhabi, United Arab Emirates. (AP Photo/Bernat Armangue)

Riquelme, in a moment of divine inspiration, looks into the stands and sends the ball exactly where it needed to go. And he sees the unmarked 'Conejo' Saviola punish Tizie with his first touch. He watches as the 'Elephants' (Ivory Coast) fight back and try to create chances without getting a goal – they only manage it towards the end, thanks to Drogba as usual – penetrating the Argentine defence, led by the impeccable Ayala. The result: 2-1. The Albiceleste look promising, even without Leo. Commenting on the game, Pekerman remarks: 'To me, football is always the same. I have expectations of this squad from an analytical point of view, not based solely on desire. We put up a great performance in terms of defence in our first match, holding off dangerous Ivory Coast players. True, we lacked presence. But the good thing is that we never lost our nerve.' It does not take much reading between the lines to realise that he is satisfied with how things have gone, which is obvious given that, in the second match against Serbia and Montenegro – which concerns him, despite the fact that they have lost to Holland – he has no intention of changing his teamsheet, except to put Lucho González in place of Esteban Cambiasso. In short, at the Gelsenkirchen stadium on 16 June, Messi is on the bench again. He has Carlos Tévez to keep him company, and 65 minutes to witness three goals and wonder how many he could score. Then he is on his feet, in his fluorescent outfit, warming up along the touchline. The warm-up is a promising sign. He returns to the dugout, following gestures and instructions, and finally assistant coach Hugo Tocalli lets him put on the blue number 19 shirt. His World Cup debut comes in the 74th minute. He comes on for Maxi Rodríguez, joining the game at the same time as Carlos Tévez, the other youngster on the team.

In the stands, Maradona lifts his arms in the air, screaming and cheering along with the thousands of Argentine fans.

They sing: 'Olé, olé olé olé, Me-ssiiiii, Me-ssiiiii!' Someone holds up a poster with the Flea's face next to the World Cup trophy. Underneath it says: 'This is my dream.' Others wave a placard that reads: 'He's Argentine and he's the Messiah.' The demand of one little girl brandishing a placard – 'José, let Messi play (please)' – is finally answered.

Up until now the Albiceleste have been playing well, no complaints, but when the Flea comes on things change: the number 19 forces a team who were starting to rest on their laurels to wake up, he gets them moving again, he makes them start accelerating more and more. They pass him the ball and he's off like a shot, with the sole objective of making it to the opponents' goal. He creates quite a spectacle as he skips along. A free kick is taken quickly and Leo is onto it, zooming along on the left-hand side of the penalty area. He reaches the line, lifts his head and slides the ball in front of the goalposts in a perfect position for Crespo who, anticipating the Serbian defence, stretches out his foot and takes the total number of goals to four. In the 87th minute Tévez passes to Crespo, who passes back to Tévez who, after having scored the fifth goal, shows his generosity by sending the ball down to Messi, who is motoring up the right wing. He gets past the defender and scores the sixth goal, sliding the ball between the post and the goalkeeper's hand. Then he pauses to point to the player who gifted him the goal. Crespo rushes over to hug him, the crowd goes wild.

This time it is a fantastic World Cup debut, although as usual the man in question plays it down: 'I wasn't thinking about my debut. I was thinking about winning a match that I really wanted to play in. In all honesty I still haven't thought about the fact that I'm now a World Cup player and that I fulfilled a dream today.' And now? Now Pekerman has a decision to make, a dilemma to resolve. 'His country wants him to play Messi from the start. And not to wait until the 74th minute. And the press, who see what sells, want it too. And, my dear friends, what press and what country wouldn't want it?' writes Pep Guardiola in *El País*. 'Only he (Pekerman) knows what he is going to do with this genius. No one doubts that Messi will give him the same over 90 minutes that he gives in fifteen. Yesterday was like that sweetie that a mother keeps hidden in her bag, well hidden, ready to give to her child when he won't stop crying. And it always works, even if only for fifteen minutes.'

At the end of the day the decision is not so difficult, the hot potato burns less because the last match in Group C against Holland is insignificant. Both teams have already qualified for the last sixteen, now they are just playing for first position in the group. Pekerman can kill two birds with one stone: Tévez and Messi in the starting line-up, Saviola and Crespo rested to avoid any yellow cards that could mean missing the next match. In the end, everyone is happy – especially those who want to see the little genius from Rosario play again.

On 21 June at the Waldstadion in Frankfurt, Lionel is awaited by Johan Cruyff, Michel Platini, Franz Beckenbauer and, of course, Diego Armando Maradona, dressed inevitably in his Albiceleste shirt. In other words, the crème de la crème of World Cup football.

Leo is the last to disembark from the team bus, iPod headphones in his ears, the last to change, after having a look at the pitch and chatting with fellow Barcelona players from the orange-clad team (Van Bronckhorst and Van Bommel) and the last to start his warm-up. When the time comes to go on the pitch, he waits respectfully in line. On his feet, he is wearing a pair of Adidas boots designed especially for his World Cup appearance. On them is his name, the sun from the Argentine flag, the phrase 'The Hand of God' and a date: 22 June 1986. The following day it will be twenty years since Diego scored two goals against England in the 1986 World Cup, one with the hand and one with the foot.

Expectation is mounting in the stands. What wonders will Lionel have for them this time? If he wreaked havoc in fifteen minutes, who knows what he will do in 90. And even if this isn't his night, the effect of his presence on the pitch is almost palpable. In the first half he plays along the right wing, marked by Tim de Cler. He has eleven touches, losing the ball once and making seven good passes. In the second half he switches to the left wing, where he is marked by Kew Jaliens. In 23 minutes he only gets three touches, only one of which is played the way it should be. In the 69th minute Pekerman substitutes him for Julio Cruz. There is very little of note: an inoffensive left-footed kick and one or two brilliant passes – one deep to Cambiasso, intercepted with difficulty by Van Der Saar, an incredible ball to Maxi Rodríguez and a beautiful 'one-two' with Riquelme with a final shot that ends up going just wide.

It was the most highly anticipated match of the first stage of the World Cup, a clash between two powerful teams with many great precedents (the 1978 final being among those that stand out), which, nonetheless, was disappointing. Some journalists maliciously imply that the number 19's rather ordinary performance will give Pekerman the perfect excuse to put him back on the bench. And back he goes.

On 24 June, his nineteenth birthday, he is back to being a spectator for 84 long minutes. And this time Argentina are not doing well: Mexico, coached by the Argentine Ricardo La Volpe, have pushed them against the ropes. When Messi comes on for Saviola, the score is 1-1. The game is heading into extra time. And it is then that the boy from Barça changes the team's rhythm, he gives it the necessary depth and sends the ball from foot to foot, building up to an amazing Maxi Rodríguez goal. Albeit with more difficulties than anticipated, Argentina have made it into the quarter-finals.

In Berlin, on 30 June, they face host team Germany. There are 120 minutes of play, of which Leo Messi plays not even a single minute. It is a mystery, the polemic of a match that ends with Argentina losing on penalties (4-2, after a 1-1 scoreline at the end of extra time).

Let us rewind the film of that decisive match, in order to understand how it is that the player who could have played a crucial role in winning the World Cup ended up on the bench.

Pekerman replaces Saviola with Tévez in the starting line-up, and Lucho González also starts. Two players who work well with the team – no complaints there. Pekerman is forced to make his first substitution in the 71st minute, when Pato Abbondanzieri is injured in a skirmish with the giant Germans. Leo Franco comes on in his place. The next to come off is Riquelme – 'he was tired', says the boss. Cambiasso replaces him. The manager is trying to achieve a balance, or rather, he is trying to bolt the door and defend the scoreline. Argentina are winning 1-0 thanks to a header from Ayala, but the players are continually trapped in their own half and they blame the Germans for the hard blows they receive. In the 79th minute the final substitution is made with Cruz coming on for Crespo, just moments before Klose heads in the equaliser. To rectify the situation would have required speed, skill and creativity, which Cruz does not possess and which Tévez can no longer muster due to tiredness after playing for the length of the match. Essentially, they needed Messi. Popular consensus seems to be that if he had come on, Argentina would have sealed the match before it got to the penalty shoot-out stage. He would have taken charge of transforming the situation.

Why didn't Pekerman send him on? Why did he choose Cruz over him? 'In that moment we needed a striker in the box and that's not Messi,' he explains in the press room after the tears, after the fight between Oliver Bierhoff, Frings and Cruz, and before announcing his resignation. 'We were always considering him [Messi] as a good option, I knew we could count on him,' says the manager. A statement reinforced by his comment that 'Argentina may have had alternatives, but we could not instigate them'. Hugo Tocalli today confirms that version. 'In order to counteract Germany's play in the air it was important to send on Cruz. We were winning 1-0 in a match we were controlling well, in which we had dominated, and then Abbondanzieri's unfortunate injury ruined all our plans.' But his explanations do not convince anyone, and one by one various theories emerge on the topic:

1. Mistake: Pekerman simply got it wrong. He misinterpreted the game, he made a hurried decision and he made the change when he should not have done so.
2. Mystery: Only the manager will ever know the truth and it will go down in Argentine footballing history as one of its many secrets, like Rattín's sending off in England in '66, Maradona's drug-taking in the United States in '94, or the red card against Ortega in France in '98.
3. Bad advice: Pekerman let himself be influenced by the heavyweights in the dressing room, who were annoyed by Messi dominating the media spotlight. In other words, Messi says he wants to play and this irritates team leaders like Juan Román Riquelme and the captain, Fabián Ayala, who ensure their feelings do not go unnoticed and call him to order at a press conference. They are the ones who convince the coach to leave Messi out of the starting eleven.

4. Etiquette and values: Pekerman could not erase or ignore etiquette, values and players who had earned their right to be on the pitch over many years.

Whatever happens, no one will ever know which of these theories is correct. José Pekerman remains silent and does not revisit the subject. A year later, in an interview with sports magazine *Marca*, when they ask: 'What happened with Messi? Wasn't there some sort of dispute over him?' he replies: 'I am proud of him and I was the one who included him in the Under 20 team when no one knew who he was. In Argentina the problem is that we have so much faith that just a little bit of Messi gets us very excitable. And people were expecting Messi to be the great Maradona of this World Cup. And he was just taking his first steps with Argentina, a great team. I hope this experience will serve him well in the future.'

And Leo Messi? He also stays silent on the topic. That night in Berlin he is one of the few who does not appear before the cameras and microphones. It is not only due to his disappointment over being knocked out of the tournament, but also because he is angry at what some of the press are saying about his behaviour during the penalty shoot-out. 'They said things like that I didn't care if we went out – which could not be further from the truth. If anyone had been inside the dressing room,' he confesses in an interview with *Mundo Deportivo* five days later, 'they would have realised what I was feeling at that moment.' He will not be drawn on the issue of Pekerman giving him so little in the way of opportunities. 'He decided that was the way it was going to be ... He did it that way because it had been working. Players like Saviola and Crespo had been doing really well, and that's that.'

That's that. Time to turn the page.

Chapter 24

Positive discrimination

Conversation with Jorge Valdano

When he is asked how he wants to be introduced, he replies, 'ex-footballer'. This despite the fact that he is currently the Real Madrid general director; and aside from winning one world championship in an Argentine shirt, he has been many other things in his lifetime: coach, sporting director, writer, commentator. Words are without a doubt among his best weaponry; metaphor is his indispensable tool; he considers analysis a pleasure.

Let's talk about Messi, a footballer who started out at Newell's, like you. Let's begin at the 2006 World Cup. An entire nation had pinned their hopes on him and instead he didn't even set foot on the pitch in the decisive match. Why?

'Pekerman is a man who knows talent when he sees it and he has never kept it hidden away. We can try to imagine that there was some problem we don't know about, probably a physical issue. Maybe he wasn't at his peak. That said, I'm with those who thought it was a shame that Argentina collapsed without Messi. In the last match many things happened: Abbondanzieri was injured, Riquelme got tired, Argentina were 1-0 up – all factors that penalised Messi. The match seemed under control. Germany were not getting anywhere, but the truth is that in their desperation to equalise Messi could have taken advantage of the opposi-

tion's disorder to score another goal. But these are all spec-
ulations, I prefer to deduce that Pekerman's thoughts are
worth more than mine because he was dealing with the facts
on the ground.'

And while we're on the topic, there has been much talk about
Messi's youth, his maturity, the etiquette of Argentine football and
the dressing room ...
'Maradona played in his first World Cup when he was 21
and it was not a happy experience. He was not entirely
mature enough yet. With Messi there was positive discrimi-
nation: we were thinking that if he had played he would
have turned the match around ...'

Now that we have dealt with that topic, let's talk about Messi and
Maradona.
'Maradona's game was more nuanced. Diego could finish
but he could also be the strategist. Messi is more intense
than that. With his assets, his physical, mental and technical speed, he is always tempted to go for the goal. Diego
sometimes used to put his foot on the accelerator, whereas
Messi lives with the pedal to the floor. It's a youthful sin.
As Menotti used to say, he needs to learn to be Joe Bloggs,
a "Jack of all trades". He can't always be Messi, because if
you're continually explosive then the opposition will have
their guard up constantly and it's more difficult to surprise
them. Their similarities? The same thing happens with Leo
that used to happen with Maradona, he's an individual who
carries such weight that he can manage without the team.
He's not like Zidane or Platini, who need the team around
them in order to display their collective intelligence. Messi
needs his team-mates to pass him the ball, after that he does
the rest on his own. Their differences? Physicality. Diego
came to Napoli eight kilos heavier and he was still a decisive

influence. Messi's game requires him to be explosive, so it is imperative he stays in perfect shape. Look at the injuries he has sustained: it seems like his muscles break him because of the amount they require of him.'

What do you think of Messi today?
'He has matured. He has a natural ability to deal with the competition. He gives the impression of being happy whenever he has the ball at his feet – he is not conditioned by context, nor by the expectation he has generated. And that is the mark of a great player, not getting stage fright. At the crossroads of his career, where you can really measure the limits of his personality, he has given us some astounding performances. We're dealing with someone who plays incredibly attractive football, and who, even with three men marking him, with his back to the goal and hemmed in at the corner flag, can be dangerous.'

What will his future hold?
'I would have liked to have had his future ... he has every reason to become the first great player of the twenty-first century. The twentieth century was carved out by Pelé, Maradona, Cruyff, Di Stéfano. He could dominate this decade, along with Cristiano Ronaldo. He's in the best possible position. Mother Nature has given him all the tools he needs. Now, he must take charge of that talent. He has an advantage: he looks at himself with a certain sense of distance. In addition, the off-pitch Leo doesn't make the headlines – that only happens when the ball is at his feet. That's another difference between him and Maradona. Diego was doubly attractive: on the one hand as a footballer and on the other as the rebel, the provocateur. He was always a volcano on the edge of erupting.'

Any advice to finish with?
'Messi has to live for the moment and relax to an extent, he shouldn't be in a hurry to be the best in the world or the one who wins the most titles. It's true, football lives maniacally for the present, but Leo has to let time play its part.'

Chapter 25

The devil

10 March 2007

Barcelona – This time, Don Fabio's nightmare is about a nineteen-year-old boy, Leo Messi. An Argentine flea who ruins his party. Capello had never won on Barça territory (not with Juve, nor with Roma, nor with Madrid), he was getting there, against all predictions. And then along came the little guy, once, twice, bringing the scores level each time and, just when it looked like it was going their way, in the 90th minute he pulls the most beautiful sequence out of his hat, the speediest dribbling, a cross into the centre: 3-3. Capello and his men are like children who have had their lollipop snatched from their mouths.

What is indisputable is that the Spanish derby has been strange, exciting, volatile, full of goals. It begins with the two captains, Puyol and Raúl, who take to the pitch and make the sign of the cross. They need it: Barça must wipe the expulsion from the Eden of Europe from the memories of the Nou Camp's 98,000 spectators, while Real Madrid is playing a game of survival – their last chance to stay in the running for the league title. The standard prediction is that the ball will be controlled by the Blaugrana, the favourites, spread across the pitch in a daring 3-4-3 formation, so that Madrid are even less marked than usual. Very few are prepared to wager a bet because Capello's men like to get their own way against their eternal rivals. And, against predictions, within five minutes they are already dominating the scoreboard. The blond Guti passes to Higuaín along the left wing. The young Argentine plays an apparently innocuous ball: it is Thuram who turns it into a lethal one, with an incredible clearance that lands at Van Nistelrooy's feet. The Dutchman takes a shot from outside the box. Pathetic diving from Puyol and Valdés. It's in – 1-0. Now it's Rijkaard's turn to be nervous. Leo Messi comes on after just five minutes. Xavi sends him a deep pass, leaving only Casillas between the Argentine and the goal. The Whites are left rooted to the spot. Equaliser.

The defenders on both sides are foundering. One of the most nervous on the Barça team is Oleguer: he is to end up being sent off in the 45th minute after receiving his second booking (for a foul on Gago). The first comes in the twelfth minute, when he grabs Guti inside the box. Penalty and yellow card. Van Nistelrooy makes no mistake. Fabio Capello cannot believe his eyes. The president told him not to come away with a defeat, but to be in the lead gives him a proper chance to breathe.

It doesn't last long. Leo Messi is proving a nightmare again, as he latches onto a rebound from Casillas. It's not easy, but he scores anyway. In under the crossbar. Credit for the equaliser must go to Ronaldinho, however, who has finally awoken from his daze. He does what he does best, unbalancing two or three opponents, doing a one-two with Eto'o and shooting at Casillas, who manages to get a hand to it at first, but can do nothing about Messi's sudden rebound. Four goals in 27 minutes: this is the type of spectacle that the Spanish crowds love. Relieved of their fears, Barça seem to take charge of the situation.

The Whites' defence is wavering, then comes the sending off, followed by a second half with only ten men. Rijkaard takes off Eto'o and sends on Sylvinho. The Blaugrana maintain control of the ball, but the Whites are dangerous. The advantage hangs by a thread. Guti takes a free kick: Sergio, Ramos and Puyol go up to meet the ball. The White defender gets a touch on the nape of his neck, the ball flies under the bar and into the back of the net. Victory? No, along comes Messi to save Barça and keep Madrid at arm's length. And Capello is back to the same old problem.

Luca Caioli, *Corriere della Sera*, 11 March 2007

Yes, Capello ... at best he had forgotten what Messi was capable of doing. And yet in the final of the Joan Gamper Trophy on 24 August 2005, it was precisely he who had asked about that devil (as he described him) who had driven the Juventus defence crazy, provoked three yellow cards, created one goal, and looked dangerous throughout the 90 minutes. At the end of the match, decided on penalties, Juventus had gone home with the cup thanks to six shots on target from the penalty spot. But Leo had been chosen as player of the match and was the genuine surprise of the game. Fabio Capello, who had instantly recognised the youngster's talent, joked with Frank Rijkaard, saying: 'Well ... if you don't have room for him in your starting line-up, give him to me, we're ready to sign him.'

Perhaps Fabio Capello thought everything would turn out well for him on the evening of 10 March 2007, just as it had on 22 October 2006 at the Bernabéu. 2-0 to the Whites and everyone at home happy, with a Messi who had put in a good effort for at least 70 minutes, with a repertoire of left-footers, assists that were wasted by his team-mates, and breakthroughs into the box. And all while receiving a series of forceful tackles from Emerson that pushed the regulations' boundaries. To the extent that, by the end of the match, he would be diagnosed with a sprained right ankle in the external lateral ligament, which would keep him out for a week.

But he hadn't managed to score.

This time the tables are turned. Has Messi got something against Don Fabio, who is currently the England manager? Absolutely not. Is it that playing against Capello brings him luck? Not that either. It's a different issue altogether. 'Playing against Real Madrid,' says Messi, 'is always particularly motivating for any player.' That is a fact and he has demonstrated it since the first time he set foot on the Bernabéu ground on 19 November 2005.

Everyone remembers that match because of the show put on by Ronaldinho (two incredibly stunning goals, not to mention everything else he did) but also because of the 'standing ovation' given by two Real Madrid supporters to the Barcelona number 10. That was undoubtedly the photo opportunity of the match. Unforgettable. It was shown on all the TV channels. Editors and journalists even went as far as tracking down the two men, one with a black moustache, the other with a beard, who were on their feet applauding. The media people wanted to know why they paid such tribute to him. Their response? How could they not applaud a superstar and his magic, even if only as a sporting gesture? But as well as the Gaucho (Ronaldinho), the people in the stands were also very impressed with Leo's performance.

Let's take a quick look at the highlights from that day. In the third minute, Sergio Ramos feels obliged to knock down the Flea on the edge of the area, in front of goal. In the fifteenth minute, Leo is the one who, after a fantastic piece of footwork, provides Eto'o with the chance to score the first goal. In the 26th minute, Messi's spectacular change of pace traps Roberto Carlos. In the 30th minute Messi penetrates the defence, but Iker Casillas blocks the shot. Barça are within reach of the second goal. In the 40th minute, Ronaldinho slaloms and crosses to Messi, but the header is wide of the goalpost. In the 47th minute Messi tries again. It's wide. A defender clears the ball. In the 55th minute Casillas denies Messi's third shot. In the 69th minute, Messi is replaced by Iniesta. These minutes and notes record that he played a fantastic game in his *Clásico* derby debut, all that was missing was the goal to take his display of speed, angles and lethal assists to the level of perfection. But the strongest memory from that match is an abundance of courage on the part of a debutant, who showed respect for nothing and nobody, who did not suffer an ounce of the 'stage fright' so beloved of his compatriot Jorge Valdano, who proved it from every part of the pitch, who took initiative and assumed responsibility, despite there being superstars on the pitch like an inspired Ronaldinho and an Eto'o on best form. These are feelings that will be widely confirmed, disputed and reaffirmed. It is a shame that he misses the return leg due to the injury he suffered at Chelsea. It is the same injury (only on the other leg) that he will sustain on 15 December 2007 against Valencia in Mestalla, five days before the classic derby. Sharp pain in the left leg, head bowed, biting on his shirt, and he's off. Goodbye classic derby. Against Real Madrid, Barça have to lose the player who made all the difference at the start of the season. The ultrasound confirms it: tear in the upper part of the femoral biceps in the left thigh. Out for four to five weeks (he will play again 36 days later, on 20 January, against Racing Santander). And he will get injured again on 4 March 2008 in the Champions League quarter-final match against Celtic in Glasgow. Another femoral biceps break in his left thigh. Another five weeks out before returning to the field.

Pause for a question: Why does Messi endure so many tears and breaks, to the point where people are already calling him 'the porcelain star'? Accumulated muscle fatigue, an old injury that has not properly healed, an insufficient warm-up, psychological stress, an imbalance of pressure on muscular areas, bad posture throughout one's career, direct impact, a supposed difference in length between one leg and the other ... there are many possible causes of injury. Furthermore, the complexity of the hamstring structure makes it difficult to pinpoint the causes and that in turn makes a player's recovery more difficult. In Messi's case, some people also factor in his physical particulars, his muscular and bone structure and his growth problems, stimulated by hormones. In any event, it is difficult to establish the precise cause, even for the Barcelona medics, who have often been slated by the press over prognostic errors with regard to recovery times. 'They told me,' explains Jorge Messi, 'that his muscular mass is made up of explosive fibres, like those of a sprinter. That's what gives him his trademark speed, but the risk of a break is considerable. In any event, Leo is perfectly aware that he really needs to take care of himself.' Let's close the chapter on the issue of injuries and resume the story of the classic derby on 10 March 2007, although, admittedly, there is also an injury involved in this story. Leo has been out for nine weeks, but this time it is not because of his muscles but because of an incident during a match. On 12 November 2006, in a game against Real Zaragoza, opposition defender Alberto Zapater stamps on his foot. The fifth metatarsal of his left foot is broken. He has to go into surgery, where a pin is fitted to stabilise the fracture and he is given a skin graft to speed up the recuperation. Prior to the match in question he played some good games, 'but,' he says, 'I still hadn't scored. That was my unfinished business.' He manages to score a hat-trick, his first at the top level (he had previously scored more goals in a match, but only on a small ground of little importance) and although it doesn't seal a victory for the team it is at least enough to save Barça's skin *in extremis*. 'Because losing to Real,' he says, 'is always bloody awful.' And that's not all – a goal allows Leo to display a message (printed underneath his shirt) that reads: 'Have strength, uncle', to his godfather, who has just lost his father. It is his way of showing his full support at a difficult time. And there is another dedication made on that magical night. It comes in the form of kisses blown to Barça's emblem. After the third goal Messi runs along and repeats the gesture, because 'I owe a lot to Barça for what they did for me when they had the chance, and also to the fans for all the affection they have shown towards me, especially in these difficult few months.' Those three goals change the course of a negative season. From 10 March onwards Leo plays frequently, he doesn't waste any chances and he doesn't just score goals – he creates works of art.

Chapter 26
Jaw-dropping

Conversation with Gianluca Zambrotta

Two seasons together. Two very weak and sad seasons for Barça. And for the defender who arrived in Barcelona after having won the Germany World Cup with the *Azzurri* (the Blues – the Italian national team). But in the Nou Camp dressing room and on the pitch the current Milan player had time to get a close-up of Messi and evaluate him.

What do you think of Leo Messi?
'I think he's one of the greatest talents to come out of the last ten or twenty years. It's undisputable that he's one of the best players in the world today, especially if we take into account that he's only 22 years old and still has a lot of time to grow.'

Do you remember the Barça-Real Madrid match on 10 March 2007?
'I wasn't at the ground but Messi's performance had a big impact on me. As it did on everyone, I imagine. He had already shown us great things back in 2005 at the Bernabéu, but in last year's classic derby he outdid himself. The most surprising thing of all is that a nineteen-year-old kid could be capable of taking the weight of a team like Barça on his shoulders, which is something very rare, and ensuring they equalised again and again. And all this in an incredibly difficult fixture, agonising, tense, hugely competitive;

all derbies are like that of course, but the truth is that the one in 2007 was particularly tough. What can I say? He has exceptional abilities and, above all, a certain maturity and sense of responsibility rare in such a young player.'

And what about that goal against Getafe?
'That I did see. For me it was jaw-dropping. "How did he manage that?" I wondered. The same question that my team-mates, the coach and the Nou Camp spectators were asking. It was an incredible goal, the goal of a star. The most beautiful goal I have ever seen anyone score. It was very similar to the one Maradona scored in '86. Although, from the ground, Leo's goal seemed to be even better than Diego's.'

From the point of view of a team-mate, what is Leo's secret?
'For him there is no difference between the Nou Camp and the football ground in his hometown. They are one and the same. He doesn't feel the pressure, or at least that's how it seems. The main thing is that there is a ball involved. He's like all the great, extraordinary players I've met: when they see a ball they become kids again, excited by their favourite toy. They won't let go of it and they would never stop playing. Try to take a ball away from Messi. You can't.'

Why?
'Because he has incredible ball control, it's always glued to his left foot, he's extremely fast, he moves well in small spaces with or without the ball, like Maradona. And he'll run rings around you to show you up. You never know where he'll go next. He could go to your right, to your left, or nutmeg you. In some matches the opposition have had up to three players marking him, but in the end he has always managed to make an impact on the game. He's in a

class of footballers where, if he's on form, he'll win you the match. He's already proven it many times. Although, in all honesty, I wasn't expecting such consistency, such high-level performance game after game. We were lucky to have him on the team.'

Is he an individualist?
'Driving the ball forward, dribbling, those are trademark elements of his game – he always wants the ball because that's how he has fun and how he entertains everyone else. It's like, when you play football with your friends and you're good, you always want the ball because you want to be the best and leave everyone astounded. No, he's not an individualist. He has grown and he knows what it means to play in a team.'

And what was he like in training and in the dressing room?
'He's a modest kid, very willing to work hard, he feels that he still hasn't reached his full potential. He's a fun guy, he jokes and fools around. He's one of those players who help to create a good atmosphere in the dressing room, one of camaraderie and friendship. He and I are not especially close, because there's a ten-year age gap, but we chat often. He seems like a mature kid who has his head firmly screwed on. With a great personality.'

Chapter 27

Leo and Diego

18 April 2007

'Barcelona Football Club are regaining ground.

Xavi ...

Messi swerves round Paredes.

He's hanging onto the ball, he's gone past Nacho as well.

Messi makes it all the way to Alexis, still with the ball.

Inside the box ... he swerves again.

The ball looks like it's going wide ...

Messi scores!

What a goal!

He has left four Getafe players and the goalie in the dust.

A right-footed shot. Nothing like the usual Messi!

Just look at that goal!

It's the 28th minute, midway through the first half.

Without a doubt, that could be the goal of the season ...

Amazing. The whole world is smiling and does not know what to make of that display of drive, speed, ability, dodging and finish. It really was truly impressive ...

I don't want to compare, but it reminds me of Diego Armando Maradona's goal against England in the 1986 World Cup. They are two different goals. They are two different players. I don't mean to say that Messi is Maradona, but it reminds me of that goal.'

That was the TV commentary of the Barcelona-Getafe game, on 18 April 2007, on Digital +.

And this is the voice of Víctor Hugo Morales on Radio Argentina on 22 June 1986 at the Argentina-England game, Azteca stadium, Mexico City.

'Diego's turn.

Maradona has the ball.

There are two men on him, Maradona's on the ball, the world footballing genius heads to the right, he gets past the third and there's only Burruchaga left to face him ...

It's all Maradona!

Genius! Genius! Genius! C'mon c'mon c'mon c'mon and

Goaaaal! ... Goaaaal!

Spectacular!

Viva!

What a goal!

Diegoal! Maradona!

Please excuse me, I'm quite emotional ...

Maradona makes a memorable run, the best play of all time ... cosmic kite ... What planet did you come from? To leave all the England players by the wayside, so that the country would be a clenched fist screaming for Argentina ... Argentina 2, England 0.

Diego! Diego! Diego Armando Maradona ...

Thank God for football, for Maradona, for these tears ...

For this score, Argentina, 2; England, 0.'

The shirts are different. So is the importance of the two games: one is a Copa del Rey semi-final, the other was a World Cup quarter-final against an opponent like England, whom Argentina were facing for the first time since the 1982 Falklands War. Although everyone denies it, non-footballing factors are making themselves felt, quite substantially ... at least in the hearts of the fans.

The protagonists are different: Maradona, the cosmic kite, is 25, he is God, he is the world superstar. When the Golden Boy scored that goal, Messi the Flea still had not been born yet. He is a nineteen-year-old kid who debuted in the Spanish league and with the Albiceleste less than two years previously.

The excitement of the commentators is incomparable: the tears, the epic feelings and the South American rhetoric versus the rigour, at least on this occasion, of the Spanish commentators, and yet ... the two goals are really quite similar, very similar, one seems to have been learned from the other. The first impression is correct.

The next day, the whole world sees history repeating itself. On global video archive YouTube, the goal unsettles Internet users. It is viewed thousands of times, as well as alongside Maradona's goal. It opens up an online debate as to which of the goals is better. Everyone has their own opinion, from expert ones to impassioned ones, while the media compares the two clips from every possible perspective, praising Leo's performance.

Headlines, commentaries and linguistic inventions of all shapes and sizes are to be heard and read: from 'Messidona', to 'The Foot of God', or even, 'Messi shocks the world'. There is no bias to speak of: the evidence is enough for even the Madrid sports papers, who are generally reticent about dedicating the front cover to their eternal rivals Barcelona. This time, however, they do not hesitate. The *Marca* front page headline reads: 'Twenty years, ten months and 26 days later, Messi repeats Maradona's goal.' And inside are quoted Víctor Hugo Morales' words: 'What planet did you come from?' It has not escaped anyone's notice that this is one of those events rarely seen on a football pitch.

Take the 53,599 Nou Camp spectators, for example: they are on their feet, grabbing hold of anything that can be waved, from the newspaper to the programme, a hand-kerchief or a scarf, waving *en masse*. And those who do not have anything of the appropriate colour still partake of the collective ritual, applauding until their hands hurt. A full-blown tribute.

Or take those who are on the pitch, like Eto'o, Deco, Gudjohnsen. The three of them hold their hands up to their faces. 'Oh my God, what did he just do?!' is the best translation of their disbelieving expressions. And it doesn't end there – in the live interviews at the end of the match, team-mates and opposition alike are brimming with praise.

'It was the best goal I have ever seen in my life' – Deco.

'He has eclipsed us all' – Jorquera.

'I only hope I don't see myself on TV in 30 years' time' – Paredes.

'Words do not exist to describe that goal. From over there on the bench I was awestruck' – Güiza.

Bernd Schuster, Getafe coach at the time, does not agree, but everyone knows what the German is like. 'We should have fouled him in order to stop him, even if it would have earned us a booking. You can only be so noble.'

The debate has begun and within a day it has spread all over the world. Although football is aesthetic and fantasti-cal, some people insist on analysing it with numbers, figures and statistics.

So here they are: Leo's goal took twelve seconds com-pared to Diego's 10.8; he ran 60 metres, while in the

Azteca stadium it was 62; he made thirteen touches against Maradona's twelve; he slalomed round five of the opposition, while Maradona left six England players in his wake. The pictures of the action are superimposed, they are analysed side by side in order to compare and understand. People look for the similarities as if it were a children's game. Buenos Aires newspaper *La Nación* does it best, pointing out ten coincidences, from the spot where the play begins right up to the celebration (both run towards the corner flag on the right hand side of the pitch). Websites, TV stations and newspapers launch their polls. The questions are more or less the same: which goal was more spectacular, that of the Flea or that of Diego? Which did you prefer? Which did you think was better? *Marca*'s poll attracts 55,000 respondents: 60.62 per cent prefer Messi's goal, while 39.38 per cent opt for Maradona's goal. The result is the same on the Cadena Ser radio station, although the margins are closer: Messi wins with 52 per cent to Diego's 48 per cent. *Mundo Deportivo*'s poll records an overwhelming majority in favour of the Barcelona striker: more than three-quarters of the voters. The *Olé* website users award Maradona 74.3 per cent of the vote. It was predictable, because that goal is engraved in the country's collective memory – there isn't a single household in which that goal hasn't been watched on video or DVD at least once. In Argentina they have even made a 'flickbook' with the goal of the century. It's a 'hand-held movie', you flick the pages and it is as if you are watching the film in action (in addition, the Icons of Argentina collection also includes the 'Hand of God' goal, Maradona's tricks with the ball in Villa Fiorito and Maxi Rodríguez's goal against Mexico; Leo Messi and his moment of glory are not yet part of this exclusive selection). And it should also be noted that in Argentina, Maradona is not just a footballer, but a people's hero, a living legend, a faith (the Maradonian

Church parodies religion and worships Diego as a supreme god), and a national historic icon, like José de San Martín (the general who fought for independence from Spain), Carlos Gardel (the famous tango singer), Evita, Jorge Luis Borges (the famous author) or Ernesto 'Che' Guevara. It's natural that the Argentines should feel reticent about trading him in as if he were a mere football sticker.

What is certain is that these polls perfectly illustrate the extent of the passion felt on both sides of the pond. As well as the debate over which goal is better, another question arises: that of Messi's intentions, or in other words, to quote *La Nación*, 'Was Messi trying to imitate Maradona? Was it or wasn't it a big coincidence?'

The man himself will erase all doubts. 'Perhaps the play was similar, I have only seen it once on television,' declares Messi, 'but I never thought it could be the same as Diego's goal. They told me afterwards, but at that moment I wasn't thinking about anything, only of the joy of having scored a goal.'

And there's more, when they ask him to describe his achievement, Leo describes it thus: 'I saw a gap and I went forward, as always, to get forward and try to score. The two defenders were closing in on me and I wasn't getting anywhere, so I looked for someone to play a one-two and when I saw the gap I got past. Luckily it worked.'

That air of simplicity, as if it was something normal (and deep down it is, it is part of his job), is reminiscent of Maradona in '86, or at least it is if we go by the memories of Jorge Valdano. 'Diego insists that he tried to pass me the ball various times, but he kept finding obstacles that prevented him,' he says, although he is convinced that in reality Diego 'was never willing to let go of that ball'. Valdano offered Maradona the chance to pass; in Messi's case it was Eto'o who did this. The parallels and similarities between the two goals are infinite, including the issue of the kick suggested by Schuster and supported by another Getafe defender. Listen to what 'el Negro' Enrique, who was present at the famous Azteca game, has to say. 'They say that the England players didn't try to foul Maradona. That's because they couldn't! Whenever they got there, he had already passed them.'

The same holds true in Messi's case. Let's stick with the anecdotes. In the Mexico World Cup it was Héctor Enrique who laid claim to his contribution to the goal and the previous pass; here, Xavi does the same. 'He told me,' reveals Messi, 'that with all the great goals everyone talks a lot about the goal, but he passed it to me and yet no one mentions it.' By contrast, there is no parallel whatsoever between what happened afterwards, among other things, because naturally the two situations were different. Perhaps there is not even any link between the words of the two protagonists. After the match, Leo says that it 'wasn't a big deal' and quietly goes out to dinner with his father and his friend Pablo Zabaleta. Unfortunately, the media attention forces him to move restaurant. There are too many people waiting for him at the usual one. At a jam-packed press conference at the Nou Camp the following day, a wet-haired, recently showered Leo says into the microphones that he has slept soundly and that 'he really has not stopped to think about the goal and what it means'. He is immune to the persistence of journalists, adding that the goal doesn't change a thing. 'I don't feel any kind of pressure, I am going to keep playing and enjoying myself as I have always done.' There is one thing, however, which he does not forget: the dedication, which he had already made at the time and now repeats. 'I dedicate it to Diego. I want to send him all my support and best wishes and hope that he gets out of there as soon as possible and recovers, because that is what the whole of Argentina and all football fans everywhere want.'

Diego Armando Maradona is in hospital. He was admitted as a matter of urgency during the night of 1 April. An alcohol relapse has caused acute alcoholic hepatitis. According to his personal physician, Alfredo Cahe, he was on the brink of death. In Argentina they even announce his death. Luckily it is not the case, and during the beginning of May Maradona is discharged from the Avril neuropsychiatric clinic where he had voluntarily submitted to therapy to help overcome his alcohol dependence. The first thing he does upon leaving is to appear on the TV programme *ShowMatch* to recount his version of events and attack those who tried to bury him before his time. And during the interview with his friend Marcelo Tinelli, he also finds time to talk about Messi's goal. Let's hear from Maradona: 'Those who made that comparison were exaggerating. They really over exaggerated. To start with, my goal was more beautiful than Messi's. And what's more, I scored it against eleven internationals from England, a world champion team, and in a World Cup. Leo scored his against Getafe, in the Copa del Rey in Spain. It's not the same.' Maradona restores his goal's reputation and accuses everyone who has dared to make comparisons as having exaggerated. Months later, in an interview with *El Gráfico*, a weekly Buenos Aires sports paper, he is even harsher. 'What was the first thing you felt after seeing Messi's goal against Getafe?' they ask him. Annoyed, he replies: 'It has nothing to do with mine.' 'The circumstances no, but the action itself was similar, Diego ...' they insist. 'No, no, leave it, they are nothing alike. I scored millions of those kinds of goals in training, they're just not on tape. If we're going to talk seriously about this, don't make me say something I don't mean ...'

Unfortunately the debate doesn't end there.

It is 9 June: Barcelona-Espanyol, in the 43rd minute of the first half.

Here is the commentary that was broadcast on one Argentine TV station:

'Now it's Messi.

It's Messi who faces up to the opposition,

Messi to Eto'o in the area.

Eto'o has his back to goal and is surrounded by four defenders.

Eto'o takes the ball out wide to the touchline.

Zambrotta ...

Messi couldn't get there ...

With his hand, with his hand, like Diego.

I'll yell it anyway:

Goaaaaal!

It's Diego! Tell me it isn't! To me it's Diego. It's the same guy ...

He's reincarnated, I don't believe in that but ... he's reincarnated. There can't be so many coincidences. Explain to me how two things can happen again in such, but I mean *such* a similar way, to two different men ... Messi, or Maradona dressed as Lionel Messi, goes down, puts on a Barcelona shirt, and levels the game with his left hand.'

And for those who are still in any doubt, here's Michael Robinson's commentary from Digital +: 'He has scored two Maradona-style goals in the same season. The two against England – one against Getafe, one against Espanyol. He has repeated them both.'

The Hand of God strikes again, with all its similarities and debates. On 22 June 1986, Maradona anticipated Peter Shilton, 15cm taller than he was, coming off his line. With his jump, Messi overpowers Carlos Kameni, who is 19cm taller than he is. Despite the protests of the England players,

Tunisian referee Alí Bennaceur allows the goal when his assistant points to the centre spot. Despite the technology available in 2007 and to the Espanyol players' despair, Rodríguez Santiago also allows the goal. Maradona is reluctant to admit what everyone already knows, 'that the Hand of God was the hand of Diego! And the same hand that also stole from England.' Just after the match, Messi is only sorry that the goal 'didn't gain anything; it only won us one point' and not the league. He celebrated 'in a normal, joyful way for having drawn the match'. There is certainly no reason to be ashamed at having done something sneaky.

Diego and Lionel, Messi and Maradona, the disciple and the master. Ariel 'the Tiger' Zárate, a 29-year-old from Entre Rios, who performs in a group of four Argentine musicians, has dedicated a song to the subject, called 'El Pie de Oro llegó' ('The Golden Foot has arrived' – a play on Maradona's nickname 'El Pibe de Oro', meaning Golden Boy). It goes like this:

On 24 June in '87
A year after Argentina became champions
A star was born, a new dream
The Golden Foot was born in Rosario.

With a magical dodge, a great, little player
At seven in the juniors for Newell's Old Boys
Over here they turned their back on his problem
And he had to emigrate and go to Spain,
He made his second home in Barcelona
And he made it, thanks to sacrifices and love.

In 2004 he debuted with Barça
And his dream was realised with the Under 20s
(The Golden Foot has arrived!)

(Chorus)
Go for it Lionel
The world is waiting to see you run again.
We want to see the magic in your feet.
(repeat)

He has a heart as big as a lion
When he comes on there's hope
The fans want to cheer his goal
In a match with the sky-blue and whites,
We cheer you on from every corner,
The national team are hopeful,
We want to see you with Argentina, as champion!

(Chorus)

Passion is awaking throughout the world
We want to see you with Argentina, as champion!

Now Messi has his own songwriter, just as Maradona had El
Potro Rodrigo. Apart from songs, the similarities between
the two have been talked about and written about numerous times, too many to count, even before that April 2007
goal. Lionel has always been compared to Maradona in one
form or another. The first to draw parallels were his Newell's
coaches, from Enrique Domínguez to Ernesto Vecchio, via
Adrián Coria. 'I have seen him do stunning things with the
ball, which not even Maradona could do at that age,' insists
Vecchio. Guillermo Hoyos, his coach in the Barcelona
youth B team, makes the same point. 'Messi is the closest I
have seen to Diego. In drive, in determination. Leo single-
handedly altered the outcome of dozens of games! He is
like Diego, they attack him, they attack him again and he
keeps going practically from the ground. You'd have to kill

him to stop him. He has no problem handling himself. The ball gets carried along by the arch of his foot and the only thing he has to worry about is speed. He already has a good feel for the ball and he does it in a different way to everyone else.'

Since then there have been many who have talked about it, in every stage of the Barça number 19's career. River Plate ex-number 10 Norberto Alonso says, for example: 'There are things about him which remind me of Maradona. Like the way he bursts forward explosively. And the speed with which he plays. But Diego had that game-altering vision which Messi lacks.'

Arsenal coach Arsène Wenger has no doubts. 'Messi is like Maradona but with a turbo attached to his feet.' Nor do footballers past and present, like Eto'o: 'Messi is the Diego Armando Maradona of the future', or Deco: 'He reminds me a lot of Maradona. Sometimes I hear people say that he should beware of the fame so that what happened to Diego doesn't happen to him. But Leo's situation is different, because he is in a healthy environment in which he is loved and protected.' And Franz Beckenbauer: 'When we see him run with the ball we are reminded of Diego Maradona at his best, with good reason.' Some do not deny the parallels, but they have words of warning for Messi. 'Between Messi and Maradona,' maintains Héctor 'El Negro' Enrique, '86 World Champion with Argentina, 'there are two things they have in common: their running style and their speed. Diego has that run and that short sprint, which makes mincemeat of you, and it's difficult to take the ball off Leo. On top of that, he doesn't just shoot for the sake of shooting, rather, he looks for the far post and dodges from right to left like Diego. The bad thing is not that he's compared to Maradona, but that Leo believes he is Maradona.' Something that also concerns Gabriel Batistuta.

The ex-Fiorentina striker and highest-ever goal scorer for Argentina says: 'Leo shouldn't try to imitate Maradona, he only has to be himself and do the best he can. Because otherwise, even if he reaches Diego's level, he will only be seen as the second Maradona.' The discordant voices are few in number, one of them being Pelé, although it is fairly natural bearing in mind the issue relates to Maradona. *O Rei* ('The King' – Pelé's nickname) is convinced that 'Messi is a different guy. Maradona used to come from behind. Messi is a bit quicker. On the other hand Diego was a better armed footballer.' Another discordant voice is that of César Luis Menotti, 'el Flaco', selector of the Argentine World Cup 1978 team. 'He is not the new Maradona. In Argentina, and in other countries as well, every time a kid comes along who has good technical skills and abilities and who is decisive, the whole world declares him as the next Diego. Messi is a very good player, left-footed, skilled, powerful, he plays for Barcelona and he's Argentine. But he is not Maradona, he is Messi.' Writer, journalist and psychologist Walter Vargas is categorical, maintaining in his book, *Football Delivery*: 'Messi is not and never will be Maradona. I say he will not reach those heights, and I even think that it will be difficult for him to come close.' There are many contrasting opinions. But there's more: the Argentine Olympic Committee even carries out a study, overseen by Miguel Toderi, in order to scientifically compare the two players. The result? A truism. They show that Messi and Maradona share a series of physical traits: low centre of gravity, muscle mass, height, weight, development and, of course, they are both left-footed.

In these cases it is better to leave science to one side and stroll through La Boca, Buenos Aires, around the Bombonera (the Boca Juniors ground), to chat to fans great and small. Rodrigo, in his blue and yellow Boca Juniors shirt, does not want to hear or speak of the matter. He has seen

Maradona play and he won't hear of any comparisons. He lists Messi's weaknesses, from his taking of free kicks to his vision of the game, and he glorifies Maradona's gifts, asking his inquirer if he remembers the number 10's first goals with the Argentinos Juniors. Let's move on to Luis, who has a photo of Maradona in action in his completely *bostero* (Boca fan) shop, with the inscription, 'Your children and your children's children will ask about him.' But then, while walking through the streets, you see some little kids playing with a ball. Two of them are wearing Barcelona shirts with Messi's name across their backs. Julián, aged ten, the most chatty of them all, says emphatically: 'I'm a Boca fan, but I like Messi, I like the way he plays.'

Perhaps preference has to do with age? 'In one of his most beautiful verses, *El Poeta murió al amanecer* [*The poet died at dawn*], Raúl González Tuñón writes: "Some people, the oldest ones, denied him from the start. Others, the youngest ones, denied him later on." That is what happens in the footballing world generation after generation. And the same thing happens to Messi,' explains Horacio Del Prado, commentator for Radio Nacional in Argentina. 'The old folks who maintain that Messi will never reach the level of Maradona forget what everyone always says when a new superstar appears: he'll never make it. They said that Maradona was chubby, too small and that he would never become a champion at the level of the greats. The great goalie Hugo Gatti was one of the ones who talked incessantly about how round Maradona was, and Diego scored four goals against him.'

Let's leave opinions aside and examine other reasons for the perpetuation of the comparison. It's simple: ever since Maradona retired in 1997, the Argentines – and others too – are always in search of a successor. It's not unusual, it always happens when a great player goes. First, time is needed in order to accept the dissolution of the myth, then time is needed in order to find someone who is reminiscent of them, who makes us relive the lost magic. And who makes us think back to old times – because memory is a fundamental aspect of football; because in order for a young player to sell, it is easier to hang a tag around his neck saying 'New Pelé' or 'New Maradona'. That way everyone knows what we're talking about. Often they get it wrong, the name designation doesn't work, or the candidate for successor does not fulfil all the promises. As was the case, just in terms of 'New Maradonas', with Ariel Ortega, Pablo Aimar, Juan Román Riquelme, or the 'Apache' Tévez. It is a difficult crown to bear. Even more so when there are so many coincidences, as there are in Messi's case: little; left-footed; grew up at Newell's, where Maradona spent a brief stint; matured at Barcelona, the first European club to experience 'Maramondo'; Under 20 world champion, like Maradona in 1979. And debuted with the national team against Hungary, exactly like Diego. And it is even more difficult when Maradona himself invites you onto his TV programme, *La Noche del 10* (*Number 10 Night*) and singles you out as his heir. 'Leo has been chosen to be one of the greats. Many think that he already is, but in my opinion,' says Maradona, 'he has hardly begun playing. He can give even more than he has already given and, when he does, it will be his moment.' When they ask him about it in *El Gráfico*, he responds that of course Leo is the best current Argentine player, but in response to the next question – 'Will Leo be able to overtake you?' – he offers: 'If it is for the good of Argentine football, let him overtake me.' Despite all his proclamations and blessings, the old king is reticent to concede his sceptre. It is up to the pretender to show that he will grasp it with honour.

Chapter 28
A long career ahead of him

Conversation with Frank Rijkaard

An ashtray, a packet of tobacco, a can of Pepsi and he begins to talk. The former Barcelona coach is relaxed, he has no urgent appointments and he willingly speaks at length, discussing the little boy who debuted with the first team on 16 October 2003.

You played impassioned games with Milan against the Napoli of Maradona, and you were Messi's coach for five years. In short, you are the best placed to resolve the issue: 'Is Leo the new Diego?'
'I have many memories of Maradona – those clashes with Napoli, in the Italian championship, they were historic; but when Diego played in Italy at 26, 27 years of age, he was already made. Messi is still very young, he has his whole career ahead of him. I understand why many people compare Leo to Diego. They are both Argentine, they're both little and they both have great qualities, but comparisons are always complicated. Back then, Maradona represented football. It's clear that he was, and is, football. Leo is a unique footballer, but in order to compare him to Maradona we will have to wait until the end of his career.'

And what about that goal against Getafe?
'I have seen a lot of football, many great players and many more goals ... I have to say that Leo's goal against Getafe

159

was one of the most spectacular that I have seen. It was a genuine work of art. I remember that after it happened I felt immensely happy for him, for the team, for the crowd; but, in all honesty, I wasn't that surprised.'

Why?
'Because you see it every day in training, when he's playing, you know that he can do incredible things and he's capable of doing things like that.'

Were you therefore not surprised by the discussion about the similarities to Maradona's goal in the 1986 Mexico World Cup?
'I thought it might happen. Because it's true that they are quite alike, although I think Leo accelerates even more than Maradona. Thousands of clips of the two goals were posted on the Internet, and I've seen at least another twenty similar ones.'

Let's return to Leo's debut with the first team.
'Leo was already talented when he was at the youth academy, but you have to reserve judgement. You have to wait and see because the transition into the first team is fundamental. It's the real test. Well, Leo surprised all of us because instead of encountering difficulties, his skills improved by playing with great footballers. In the Gamper [trophy], against Juve, everyone realised what the boy was worth.'

What are his characteristics, his qualities?
'It doesn't matter if he is playing in front of ten spectators or 100,000. Leo is the same as always, he always feels secure and has the same desire to win. He is the boy who says: "Give me the ball, I want to play, I want to be creative, I want to show my talents." And when he gets it, it's a difficult task to stop him without fouling him. He is extremely fast, he has

great ball control, an exquisite touch and he can dribble in a way rarely seen throughout the footballing world. And let's not forget, he's explosive, and although he's not very tall, he is very strong. You can see it when he clashes with the opposition – it's not easy to knock him down.'

How has he changed over the years?
'When he debuted he was a very well balanced person, calm, respectful and very shy. Over time, he has changed a lot, but without losing these attributes. Now he is more sure of himself, he is conscious of being an important player in the team. Everyone values him and he is perfectly aware of it. His attitude has not changed, but he is not the silent boy he was all those years ago. He is funnier, he likes to joke around when he is with his team-mates or surrounded by people he knows ... I have to say that from day one the team has behaved very well towards him, the group has accepted him. Sylvinho, Deco, Ronaldinho, they've helped and advised him. Great players always recognise a special player.'

What kind of relationship did you have with Leo?
'I care about him a lot. At the beginning, I felt he needed my sympathy and support, because of his age. Later on I saw that he needed it less: he knows what his options are, he knows how the footballing world works. He has assumed many responsibilities and he will assume many more, for his team-mates, his club, and the shareholders. He is already mature enough to do so because he has developed as a person and as a footballer, he has experienced some wonderful moments, and some very difficult ones.'

Like when he was injured against Chelsea and you hugged him as if you were his father?

'To me it was a natural thing to do. I felt his suffering, I knew how important it was to him to play in that match. Getting injured is unbearable. The only thing I could do was console him, and say: "Don't worry, you'll be better soon." It was a very emotional moment, very beautiful, although it wasn't nice at all. But you have to deal with these things in your career. They are the things that make you grow, that motivate you to keep playing, to make it to the top.'

Tell us some advice, or the most important advice, you gave Leo.

'Finish the action: shoot, or cross it, don't keep dribbling. Because there is more of a risk of losing the ball or getting injured. You can't dribble for 90 minutes, nor can you dribble past ten men and the goalkeeper in every match. You can do it once a year, not every Sunday. That's the advice I gave him years ago and it seems that he took it on board. He demonstrated as much this season: in many games he has scored one or two goals, or given a team-mate an assist. In short, he has improved his football and he is showing his maturity. He needed to, because Leo sees a lot more than others do on the pitch. He can achieve more than others. What he can't do is wear himself out pointlessly, not pace himself and not make a difference.'

Rijkaard lights another cigarette and then, continuing his train of thought, adds:

'There is a sense that Maradona used to transmit, and now Messi also transmits, the joy of playing. They are two people who have fun with a football. It seems that they are always asking for the ball ... and they're saying "Let's play".'

Chapter 29

You have to prove it

Conversation with Carlos Salvador Bilardo

Call him the oracle, the professor, the grey matter, the father of a new school of footballing thought (Bilardism, of course), or simply, the *Narigón* (nosy one). All of them are titles that Bilardo has garnered over the length of his successful career as a footballer and coach, as much in his own country as abroad. His philosophy is well known: 'Winning is all that matters,' and 'No one remembers the runner-up,' and of course 'A final is a question of life and death.' Now, after a stint in politics as sports secretary for the province of Buenos Aires, the medical doctor who dedicated himself to football has returned to his true love: he is now the general manager of the Argentine national team. And, as always, he enjoys reflecting on football in his usual frank and ironic way.

It's possible that you were the coach who has had the greatest understanding with Maradona. You had it in the national team who won the World Cup in Mexico in '86; in Italy in '90 when the Albiceleste reached the final; and in Sevilla; and now you stand at his side in the Albiceleste. In short, you know Diego very well, and you follow Messi's development, which leads us to ask: 'Is Leo the new Diego?'
'In Argentina, and not only in Argentina, when a new player breaks onto the scene there is always a comparison to be

made with Maradona. Many people have gained the title of new Maradona ... the problem is that they have to keep proving that they're on his level. In his day, Diego proved he was the best in the world. Messi is doing very well, he's on the right track, but if he doesn't win a World Cup, as team leader, he will never get to Maradona's level. Just as has happened with other great footballers who haven't been crowned world champions. I'm thinking of Gullit, Cruyff, or Platini.'

And can Messi win the World Cup?
'I'm not an oracle. All I can say is that there are a few months until the South Africa World Cup and Messi can improve a lot in every sense, technically and in terms of maturity.'

Leaving the future aside, let's talk about Messi's goal against Getafe and Maradona's goal against England, which you saw from the dugout ...
'They are two similar goals, in different situations: one at a national level in the quarter-finals of a world championship, the other at a club level in the semi-finals of the Copa del Rey.'

OK ... but did it surprise you?
'It surprised me the way that Spain went crazy for Messi. They couldn't talk about anything else. And here as well: they didn't stop showing it on TV over and over again.'

And from a technical point of view?
'It surprised me that from the moment he got the ball until the execution, Messi maintains the same level of power. Maradona changed rhythm and Messi always moves in the same way. He does the same as all left-footers who play on the other touchline. When they get the ball on the right

hand side and move inwards they have the whole width of the goal in which to score.'

Which of the two do you prefer?
'I'll stick with Maradona's goal. Maradona had people coming at him continuously, and the central defenders staggered their attack: first Butcher and then Fenwick. Messi ran 30 metres without anyone trying to tackle him. That's why he gets more touches with his right foot, his weaker foot. He leads with it, and then he always sidesteps with his left foot. It's very difficult for the defenders to get at him because he comes bounding along and he goes very fast. In the end, the central defenders wait for him in a line, and it's easier for him.'

Messi and Maradona ... let's consider their qualities.
'From three-quarters of the way up the pitch, up to the goal, they are two players who can decide a match, they have quick, short steps, it's difficult to take the ball from them and they also kick well.'

Can you compare them in other respects?
'Comparisons are an eternal feature of football. How many times has Maradona been compared to Pelé, Platini or Cruyff in order to ascertain who was better? But times are changing, just like with medicine. The knowledge of a doctor today is not the same as it was twenty years ago.'

Anything else?
'I still don't know Messi very well. With regard to Diego I can say that he is a man who knows his football, tactically and technically.'

Chapter 30
Disappointment

15 July 2007

Sadness and anger. These feelings and many more occupy Messi's thoughts and words in the middle of June. The reason is simple: Barcelona haven't won the titles they were hoping to take home. From eight possible titles, they have had to make do with the Spanish Super Cup – nothing more. A particularly poor outcome. And for someone like the Flea, who thinks only of winning, he cannot but feel bad about it. And think about how 'we started well. Then we were knocked out of the Champions League too early. Then, when we thought we had got past the most difficult part, we went out of the Copa del Rey. If you add it all up, it's painful,' he explains in an interview with *France Football*. He doesn't speak of the league, the hardest blow to deal with. In February, it seemed as if the Blaugrana had it in the bag and that the persecution of Capello's Real Madrid was nothing more than a dream to keep the championship alive and to have something to say to the media. However, it wasn't to be: points lost in the final moments, particularly against Betis and Espanyol, end up gifting the title to the Whites. Why not give a financial incentive to Mallorca, Madrid's rivals in the last fixture on 17 June at the Bernabéu? (It is common practice in Spain to reward teams who beat your local rivals.) Messi sees nothing wrong with it if it helps them win, but despite the Argentine's good intentions and expectations, the miracle, which seemed possible in the 65th minute, is not forthcoming in the end. And so, the last chance to save the season disappears, leaving only disappointment. In short, nothing has turned out as expected and 'the hero is left without a prize', as the *El País* headline reads. Because in fact, on an individual level, it has been a positive season for Messi. The Argentine has played an indisputable starring role in many magical nights: it was he who momentarily thwarted Real Madrid's inconsistencies with his famous hat-trick. Then came the Foot of Maradona and the Hand of God II, wonders and tricks that did not amount to anything. The goals scored and the award for best foreign Liga player are nothing more than a meagre consolation prize.

Luckily, football doesn't stop. Awaiting him are the national team and the Copa América and, with them, the chance to recover from the blow he has suffered. And the possibility of being in the starting line-up in an important tournament, not simply part of the squad, as happened to him in the Germany World Cup.

Alfio 'el Coco' Basile, the selector who has assumed José Pekerman's post, is counting on him. He knows that the Flea has a huge amount to contribute to the national team and that he has a fundamental role to play in his plans for the team. He does not want to repeat his predecessor's errors. He calls him up for the European mini-tour, in Berne and Barcelona, where they will face Switzerland and Algeria, with a view to playing him in the continental championship which will take place in Venezuela, where the whole world is convinced that Messi will play the leading role. In a poll on the tournament's official website, Leo is winning by a considerable margin (33 per cent of the votes), beating the Chilean Matías Fernández and the Venezuelan Juan Arango. Brazilian Real Madrid player Robinho, who will eventually be chosen as best player and will be awarded the title of highest goal scorer, with six goals, is bottom of the list with only eight per cent of the votes.

On 24 June in Maracaibo, four days before Argentina's opening match against the United States, Messi celebrates his twentieth birthday and the media wheedle out of him an obvious wish: 'To win the Copa América and be the highest goal scorer.' Argentina has not won it since 1993, making the pressure and expectations enormous. The expectations placed on Messi are so high that, in contrast to what happened in Germany, both the squad and the coach fuss over him. Coco even provides him with a mentor: 'La Brujita' Juan Sebastián Verón. The 32-year-old ex-Boca, Sampdoria, Parma, Inter, Lazio, Manchester United and Chelsea player, who has had newfound success with his first love, Estudiantes de la Plata (an Argentine team), offers advice to the twenty-year-old Messi both on and off the pitch, and defends him against accusations that he is an arrogant soloist. 'Messi is reserved. He doesn't hang out in a group drinking *mate*. He prefers to play PlayStation. To me it's like he's my little brother, who I have to take care of. I have to keep him safe!' he explains in *El País*. And in fact, Messi does need taking care of because Messimania has been unleashed in Venezuela. It's madness, the kid can't take a step without being surrounded by hordes of fans, shirts with his name on are selling like hotcakes to adults and children alike, on the pitch he barely has to touch the ball to get a standing ovation, even when he misses. If he is not in the starting line-up, as happens in the game against Paraguay, within ten minutes the annoyed crowd are calling his name.

It is a blind love, which reaches its peak at the Lara de Barquisimeto stadium. Messi is walking towards the dressing room tunnel, tired and distracted, when out of the blue he sees a girl. Leo has seen that she is about to throw herself off the stands – worried, he waves his arms and shouts: 'Stop, what are you doing ...?' The love-struck twenty-something doesn't listen to reason and jumps. Luckily she falls on her feet. Soldiers and security guards pounce on her, but before they can take her away she manages to embrace her idol and plant two kisses on him. Leo looks decidedly perplexed, as does Simon, the referee, who grabs him by the arm demanding an explanation, convinced that it was some kind of attack.

'It was unbelievable. I was signalling to her not to jump and she ended up jumping anyway. I swear I didn't know what to do,' he will later confess to *Clarín*. 'It was at least a four-metre drop. She could have killed herself, and on top of that they got her out of there pretty quickly without even seeing if the poor girl was okay or not.'

The incident happens on 8 July, in the quarter-finals. Argentina have just beaten Peru 4-0, and in the 61st minute Messi has scored that longed-for goal. He did not score in the previous matches, against the United States, Colombia and Paraguay, although he has been decisive in mobilising and transforming the Albiceleste machine. Like in the debut against the Americans, when he serves the ball up on a plate for Crespo to score his second goal, or during the 25 minutes in which he plays in the second half of Paraguay-Argentina (Basile wants to rest him for the quarters), when he brings a bit of spice to an otherwise boring game. But he was still missing the goal, and scoring it against the Peruvians is a weight off his shoulders. And in the semi-final against Mexico in Puerto Ordaz, he re-establishes his position, creating another masterpiece. According to the commentators, 'They should pack up and go home'. 'That's what geniuses do,' says Basile. 'Shall we pack up and leave? What more do we need? Why should we continue after having seen that goal?' The commentators of Tyc Sports, an Argentine TV channel, agree with Coco. And that's not all.

Here's little Carlos Tévez: 'What Messi did was brilliant. He didn't have many clear opportunities to score, but the first ball he got was an incredible goal.' Mascherano: 'It was one of those moments of genius that we've come to expect from him. Nothing he does surprises me any more. He's extraordinary.' Cambiasso: 'It was a stunning goal.' Heinze: 'There are no words to describe Messi's goal.' In essence, a goal that ended up taking its place among all the clips of the Flea's best goals posted on the Internet.

But what has he managed to pull out of his hat this time? Let's see the replay. In the 60th minute Heinze, who scored the goal that put them ahead, passes to Cambiasso. The Inter player, with two defenders closing in on him, returns it to Heinze who looks for the shot from his own half; Tévez receives it outside the box with his back to the goalkeeper. He controls it on his chest, plays it down, turns and passes to Messi who is off, quick as a flash. He gets into the box, lifts his head, sees the goalie and sends the ball through the air with incredible grace. A perfect arc, a chip which beats Sánchez, the desperate goalie, who jumps backwards and stretches out a gloved hand, but doesn't even manage to get a finger to the ball, which curls in under the crossbar. Leo watches the ball until the net billows, then he runs towards the corner flag to celebrate with the Argentine fans. Verón, his mentor, is the first to reach him, the boy jumps on his neck while from the dugout Coco throws up his arms, applauds and laughs delightedly.

'Did you feel they should have packed up and gone home after your masterpiece?' 'No, stop it, stop it. It was a beautiful goal, nothing more. The important thing is that it helped Argentina get to the final.' That is Messi's response to the question from *La Nación* the following day. But they push him. 'Do you think it was the most amazing goal of your career?' 'Maybe, I don't know, I have scored a few good ones, like the one against Getafe. The truth is I haven't really seen it on TV. Everyone says it was really good: I saw the goalie come off his line and I took the chance. It turned out well, didn't it?'

Same old Messi, unshakable in his modesty. Although he claims the rights to his dream: that of beating Brazil in the final. Leo had said since the beginning that he wanted to play against Brazil, and his wish has been granted. He wants to put that 3-0 from a friendly at Wembley the previous September behind him.

His friend Ronaldinho will not be there, which Leo says is just as well; neither will Kaká. In any case, although they have lost the opening match against Mexico and only managed to win the semi-final against Uruguay on penalties, the Green and Golds are still tough rivals to beat. Moreover, finals are a different story – you can never be certain what will happen. Something that does become painfully certain is that Argentine dreams are buried with a resounding 3-0 thanks to the beast Júlio Baptista, Albiceleste captain Ayala's own goal, and Daniel Alves. They corner the elegant team and they do it well. At the José Romero stadium in Maracaibo, Argentina make no impact, it's as if they don't exist. And Messi? 'He did little to change history,' says *Clarín*. 'With neither frenzy nor football, Leo ended up being fenced in by his Brazilian marker and remained trapped in his labyrinth.' The images are more revealing than commentaries or critiques. Messi sitting on the pitch with a lost look in his eyes; Dady, the physio, shaking his head at him in a consolatory gesture; FIFA president Joseph Blatter presenting him with his medal, and Messi coming down from the stands only to take it off and hold it in his fist. He has been chosen as the best young player of the Copa América. But what good is that ... in the wake of this new disappointment, there is nothing but anger and sadness.

Chapter 31
An electric kid

Conversation with Alfio 'El Coco' Basile

Seated at his usual table in the back corner of the La Raya restaurant in Buenos Aires, Coco is chatting with a group of friends. Among them are players, journalists, old acquaintances – a regular get-together. Every so often, the unmistakable deep, rough voice of the Argentine coach is heard above the background hum and the noise of glasses clinking and cutlery scraping. Claudio Codina, the owner of the restaurant who is like a son to Basile, gently interrupts the gathering and joins him in talking about Messi. With a cigarette between his fingers and a glass in his hand, the words flow thick and fast from the mouth of the Bella Vista ex-defender.

'I love Leo very much, because he's a great lad. He's humble, he doesn't think highly of himself, he doesn't think of himself as a star and the fame hasn't gone to his head. He's a good person. He's the son every parent would like to have, or the one you'd want to date or marry your daughter. People everywhere love him and not just because he's an incredible footballer, but because of his personality. Incidentally, let me tell you a story.'

Tell it, tell it ... please.
'We were in Oslo, in a little field surrounded by huge buildings. It was an evening training session, almost nightfall,

and there was no one around. But something happened that you don't expect in a country like Norway, where you'd think even the football fans are cold ... All of a sudden the lights went on and the windows opened in houses around and we started to hear people yelling from all directions: "Messi! Messi! Messi!"'

And what did he say?
'Nothing ... it embarrasses him, in the best sense of the word, when people call out to him or praise him. You can see him practically suffering when the spectators shout his name. And the girls ... they go crazy, as we saw in Venezuela ... Such affection for that little face, for that shyness, for the humanity he exudes ... Those are attributes that he gets from his parents. He has an incredible family, who really protect him. When I saw his mother, she said to me: "Look after him for me Coco, please look after him for me."'

And did you look after him?
'Of course. I tried to help him, I tried to relieve as much of the pressure as possible, the way they do at Barcelona. They also protect him because they know what he means to their team. But Leo doesn't get overwhelmed by the pressure. When he gets onto the pitch he doesn't think about what's going on around him, he only thinks about playing with the football. He loves the football.'

While we're on the subject, let's talk about Messi in terms of football.
'I met him when he was only fifteen years old and I thought he was very good; now he's an outstanding footballer. He has speed, acceleration; he can dodge, he's always capable of creating something new; he is in great shape and has

enormous talent. He's an electric kid. As I always say, I find it exciting to watch Messi play.'

As you did in the Copa América when Leo scored that goal against Mexico, and you said: 'They should pack up and go home. That's what geniuses do.'
'Was I wrong?'

We don't even need to answer that ... Let's move onto another genius, Maradona, whom you know well and with whom you have shared ups and downs. Can Messi be compared to the number 10, the way everyone is doing?
'We have to wait and see. Leo is not yet Maradona. He has only just begun. He hasn't forged a career path yet. He plays a similar game, but there's no need to compare them because people will want him to play like Maradona now. He has all the right criteria to be one of the greats, but we have to wait, for now he just has to keep doing what he's doing and enjoy playing. Let's not forget that he's only 22 years old.'

When he talks about you, Messi says again and again that you put up with him from the beginning, that you always let him play and gave him a lot of freedom ...
'From three-quarters of the way up the pitch Messi has the freedom to go anywhere, freedom to be inventive, to play the way he knows best, to make challenges, to dribble up the pitch, to soar. The best players need to soar.'

Chapter 32
Bronze and silver

17 December 2007

Let's try and get our heads around the numbers: one goal in eight matches in his first season with the first team; seven goals in 23 fixtures in the 2005–06 season; fifteen goals in 31 matches between the league and the Champions League in the 2006–07 season; eight goals in the first slew of fixtures at the beginning of the 2007–08 season; 21 goals in 22 matches since he scored the hat-trick against Real Madrid in March 2007. But the figures do not do justice to Leo's progression. Instead let's take a look at the headlines:

'Messi is worth the whole team' – *El País*, 20/09/07
'Messi plays Messiah' – *Marca*, 23/09/07
'Messi dominates' – *El Mundo*, 23/09/07
'Messi's got guts' – *El Periódico*, 27/09/07
'Messi was worth the entrance fee' – *La Vanguardia*, 30/09/07
'Messi is king of La Liga' – *Marca*, 08/10/07
'Messi's irresistible rise' – *Sport*, 09/10/07
'Messi does the mambo' – *Mundo Deportivo*, 09/10/07
'Messi starts to do what Maradona did before him' – *As*, 18/10/07

And it's not just the headlines on every page which celebrate the moment of glory, the divinely inspired play, 'the brilliance and inspiration' of the Argentine 'who turns everything he touches to gold'. The comments of the coaches, the rival teams, the football experts, both Spanish and Argentine, and the studies also document his explosion. There is talk of a 'footballer without limits', and it is stated that, given his mindset, Messi is capable of 'taking risks and directing the game'. There is talk of his extreme running speed: 4.5 strides per second, which beats the 4.4 of Asafa Powell, the speedy Jamaican who set a 100-metre world record of 9.74 seconds in Rieti (Italy) on 9 September 2007. There are discussions regarding his low centre of gravity, which allow him to control and drive the ball forward with characteristic ease. Comparisons with the number 10 are made continually.

In an exclusive interview in *Marca*, Diego does not argue with any of this; he simply explains that 'if Rijkaard puts Messi on the bench, Laporta will throw him out'. And after his team's harsh defeat at the Nou Camp, Zaragoza coach Víctor Fernández says what everyone is thinking: 'Messi could be the best in the world.'

As though besieged by an avalanche, the compliments swirl around Messi from September to November. And since it's not long before the nominations for *France Football*'s Ballon d'Or and the FIFA World Player, the hopes and the voting predictions become more and more outspoken. 'Messi is close behind Kaká,' writes *La Vanguardia*. 'Messi is a candidate for the Ballon d'Or. His performance and goals for Barça and Argentina make him a favourite,' announces *Marca*. It is a full-blown campaign in favour of the Flea, although everyone is conscious of the fact that Kaká is the favourite and probably already has the prestigious award in the bag. But either way, it is better to campaign, and give some impetus to the Argentine's cause. In the meantime, while awaiting the verdict, Messi is awarded the Bravo, the prize given by Italian sports magazine *Guerin Sportivo* to the best Under 21 in the European championships. Leo is the first Argentine and third Barcelona player to win it, after Guardiola and Ronaldo. It is 25 November. Just one week later, Ricardo Izecson Dos Santos Leite, 'Kaká' (a nickname given to him by his brother), lifts the Ballon d'Or. Messi is in third place. Bronze, with 255 votes. Cristiano Ronaldo is just ahead of him with 22 more votes, while Kaká has received no fewer than 444 votes.

The Brazilian, who is a member of the Reborn in Christ Church and a fervent evangelist, gives thanks to God 'for being lucky enough to be able to dedicate myself to this profession'. He believes that Milan's Champions League victory and his position as highest goal scorer are what helped him triumph over his opponents. Of Leo, he says: 'He represents ability and control of the ball. He is young and full of talent, I think he is very good.' The difference between them? It's simple, explains Kaká, 'Messi hasn't won any important titles this season, not La Liga, nor the Champions League, and I think that has counted against him.'

It is the same story fifteen days later at the FIFA World Player Gala 2007. With just one difference, which makes one of the top players extremely nervous. Kaká takes gold again with 1,047 votes, best player of 2007 according to his colleagues; but Leo moves up to silver (504 votes), overtaking Cristiano Ronaldo who, with 426 votes, has to make do with the bronze.

It is amusing seeing what happens in the room. The presenter announces Messi in second place and Ronaldo in third. The two of them stand up at the same time in the front row of the stalls in order to go up on stage. Messi buttons his jacket. It is the first time he has ever worn a suit and he looks decidedly unaccustomed to such attire. FIFA president Joseph Blatter and Pelé do the honours on the

Zurich Opera House stage. Cristiano Ronaldo is the first to shake hands all round. He nods to O Rei and, without hesitation, picks up the second place silver trophy. Blatter has to motion to him and insist: 'Messi, it's for Messi.' The presenter repeats the result of the votes and asks them to switch trophies. An uncomfortable moment smoothed over by the presenter with a 'you did very well but you just missed it', to Cristiano Ronaldo.

The two of them change places for the photo and the ceremony continues without any problem.

'Blatter said that that one was for me; then, when I went to pick it up, it turned out that the other one was for Cristiano and this one was for me,' Leo comments at a press conference later. When asked how he feels, he replies: 'The truth is that I feel happy, all those people who voted, they gave me this prize ... Before it all happened I said that it was already wonderful just to be in the top three, so I'm very happy. It was all new to me, so I was just taking it in and enjoying it.'

Leo Messi shouldn't even have been there. The injury he picked up the previous Saturday at Mestalla had threatened his attendance at the gala. Then, at the last minute, the doctors give him a good report, so the Blaugrana expedition leaves for Zurich, headed up by Joan Laporta, who receives the FIFA Fair Play Award on behalf of FC Barcelona. Jorge and Rodrigo go along to keep Leo company.

Two days later in Barcelona, the father and brother find time to talk about their trip to Switzerland, the prizes, and various other things related to the champion they know so well. Is there disappointment that he missed out on the gold? 'Just the fact that he is second and third in the world at twenty years of age, means Leo is already a footballing icon. He still has time to make it to number one if he continues like this,' says Jorge, sipping a cup of tea. 'In all honestly,

did you ever imagine that your son would get to this level?'
'No, I never imagined he would go so far. I was betting on
Rodrigo, who was a good striker. He grew up at Newell's, he
played with Central Córdoba, he played as a reserve in the
first division, he had a motorbike accident that kept him
out for a year, he trialled in Chile, and then I brought him
here to see if he could find a Spanish or another European
team.'

'The difference,' comments his older brother Rodrigo,
'is that Leo has an attribute that I didn't have: he has a lot
of willpower, he has made a huge number of sacrifices to
get to where he is. I didn't have as much willpower. I'm a
lot more lazy.' But who instilled Leo with such a passion
for football? 'I was never one of those frustrated footballers
who wants their kids to be champions at all costs. I never
aspired to that. It was my mother-in-law who used to take
Rodrigo and Leo to play, not me,' declares Jorge. 'Yes, it's
true that I coached him for a year at Grandoli, but I wasn't
his teacher. I enjoyed watching him play.'

So then where does his passion come from? 'Back when
I used to play, I loved football,' says Jorge. 'I woke up in the
morning and went to bed at night thinking about football,
maybe that has been passed down to Leo.'

'When my brother was five or six years old,' explains
Rodrigo, 'there was no other present that could make him
as happy as a football could. He was crazy about football like
all the kids. But he knew how to be faithful to his childhood
passion and he's pursued his dream. Because his happiness
was, and still is, tied up with football.' And what does the job
involve for a factory-worker-turned-football-agent father?
'For his own benefit I have to protect him from the expectations of interested parties who could harm him. There are
people who seem trustworthy but actually they're criminals.
The world is full of them. It's not easy, I have had to learn,

I have made mistakes, and bit by bit I have straightened out any issues along the way.' How is the father-son relationship? 'Good, apart from the generational difference, which creates a barrier. I try not to smother him too much, that's what he needs. I prefer him to be surrounded by youngsters his own age, his brothers, his friends. I don't want my son to think: he's always around. If he needs advice I give it to him, if not ... I try not to get involved in anything. I tell him things and I can see that he often takes it on board. Money? Contracts? We almost never talk about those things, we chat more about football, the football here and the Argentine teams, like a get-together between friends.'

And how are things going with the older brother? 'I was by Leo's side during the first few years here, in Barcelona. They weren't easy years, we used to get very bored,' explains Rodrigo. 'They were sad times, we would spend them watching films or playing PlayStation. Then, bit by bit, his life changed, and so did mine. Every so often he likes to get off the pitch and go out to eat. In terms of nightlife? He doesn't like going out that much. I used to like going out, he would rather get a drink and have a chat. He spends a lot of time with us. He looks after Agustín a lot, my oldest child, who is turning five, and he loves my little girl, who was born in 2006. He also likes the meals that my wife Florencia makes – her roast chicken and *empanadas* could rival my mother's.'

A question for the head of the family: does all that money change a player and his family? 'We don't have luxuries, we still haven't finished the house in Rosario. Leo has a chalet here in Castelldefels: two floors, four bedrooms, a garden and a small pool. We live just as we did before, but people look at us and think we've changed; on the contrary, they are the ones who have changed. They look at us differently ... they envy a boy who has done well. The money that Leo earns is put away safely so that he and his family shouldn't have any problems in the future.'

The last question, that has to be asked, is about his son's future. 'I think it will be good. He'll keep developing, he'll be even better.' Better than Maradona? 'Diego was one of a kind. Leo is different, these are different times; I hope he comes close to the number 10's level, in terms of the technical qualities he displayed and the results he achieved.'

Chapter 33

Physical thinking

Conversation with Roberto Perfumo, 'El Mariscal'

The La Biela waiters and clientele know him well. Some of them stop and greet him and ask for his perspective on the issues of the day. Once he has dished out his opinions to all and sundry, the Mariscal – ex-defender for River, Racing and Cruzeiro, one of Argentine football's best defenders, who is also a commentator and a social psychologist – finally sits down to have a cup of coffee. The walls are covered with photos of motor racing champions like Juan Manuel Fangio, Friolán González and Manuel Gálvez, who in the 50s and 60s used to frequent this café-bar, situated opposite the famous Recoleta cemetery in Buenos Aires. Those were different times. Today, the talk is about football.

What do you think of Lionel Messi?
'Technically speaking he's one of the few players in the world who can drive the ball forward without looking at it, and that allows him to watch the opposition and his team-mates, and make an unprecedented pass. He can do it because he sees the whole pitch. He has a lot of precision while at the highest possible speed. He plays imaginatively, he's creative and every time he gets the ball, every time he challenges the opposition, it's an experience ... everyone is waiting for something to happen. And it does. In addition, for me Messi has physical thinking.'

What does that mean?
'He is mind and body. All at the same time. He has the same gift that Pelé, Maradona and Di Stéfano had. It's the speed with which his brain tells his legs what to do. Messi gets an idea and, bam! it's already happened. Do you know what I mean? Seeing the position of the goalie and shooting between the posts is done through intuition, not through thinking.'

Since you've mentioned Maradona, the obvious thing is to ask you about the comparisons that have been made and are still made continually ...
'After Pelé retired, it took Brazil another 24 years to become world champions again. We are still in mourning for Maradona. We're all hoping a Saviour will appear, the new Messiah, who will take us to the top once again. Messi could reach that position, but he still needs time, he needs to develop his gifts and prepare himself for the opposition, he needs to reach his footballing maturity.'

What are his weaknesses?
'He still has a youthful sin: he doesn't always know how to make the best choices. Sometimes you have to make a run, sometimes you have to pass, it's useless to persist when a play is not going your way, it's better to choose the most simple and effective solution. He himself will realise that it's the ball that has to keep on running ... these are things you learn with experience and with age.'

Is Messi already an icon?
'He is a simple guy, very humble, and kids admire him enormously.'

Why is that?
'Because of his look, because of his face. He reminds me of the *cuis* (a type of squirrel, one of the most common Argentine mammals). Add to that his natural magnetism when the ball is between his feet. I hope he never loses his passion for playing ball. That's the only way he will be the best in the world.'

Since you are so sure of your prediction … let's move on to talking about the future and, in particular, the risks.
'I hope that the money doesn't soften him. With millions of euros in the bank he still needs to run, train, play in the cold, the rain, the snow. I hope he doesn't become an advertising icon like Beckham; the risk is that you lose the passion for the game. I hope he never loses that "amateurism", that love of being on the pitch that guys like Pelé and Maradona preserved. Being Messi won't be easy, it will definitely be a headache. In any case, he is still climbing uphill to reach the top. The most difficult part will be once he is up there and has to maintain that level. Look at Ronaldinho.'

Meaning?
'Juan Manuel Fangio used to say, "When the bad times come, no one can endure them." That is what's happening to Ronaldinho. When things start to go wrong … you say to yourself, it's fine, I'll get back to form. But you don't look after yourself, you don't concentrate, they start to question you every blessed day, the environment doesn't help because friends of a champion are the worst kind, family is a disaster, and you keep careering downhill without being able to apply the brakes. You don't realise it and time passes. It's a lesson Messi needs to remember when he's at the top.'

Chapter 34

The long journey towards gold

22 May 2008

'I'm excited because it's the Argentine national team. And I always said that I want to play for my country. It's the Olympics ... it's an opportunity a player gets once in his career, if he gets it, right? It's possible that I might get the chance to be there and I would love to go. What if there's a conflict with the club? I don't think there will be. I think the club understands how I feel and ... there won't be any problems.'

It is just after 1.30pm on a grey Thursday. There is quite a buzz in the Hesperia Tower hotel in Barcelona, close to El Prat airport. Today sees the first gathering of the Argentine Under 23 squad. It is the beginning of an Olympic adventure for Sergio 'el Checho' Batista's boys. There is an atmosphere of reunion and re-acquaintance, between players, between players and coaches, between footballers and journalists – who have been positioned in the foyer for a while now in order to get an interview.

An exhausting initial training session is followed by a procession of white shirts towards the dining room; after the meal there is a press conference in the enormous auditorium. In theory it is only an introduction to the Catalunya-Argentina friendly, which will be played two days later at the Nou Camp, on Saturday 24 May. The adverts are promoting it as a challenge between two extremely young Barça stars

– Lionel Messi on the one hand, and Bojan Krkić on the other. But the sixteen-year-old from Linyola will not be on the pitch. Catalan selector Pere Gratacós would prefer not to play him to avoid a headache, since Bojan turned down Luis Aragonés' call for him to play for the Spanish national team in the European championship, claiming tiredness. Leo is there, however, and becomes the main protagonist before a crammed audience of Catalan and Argentine journalists. Checho is sitting beside him and observes the reporters pestering him with questions about all the issues currently facing Barcelona: the new coach, the possible departures of Ronaldinho and Deco – two team-mates with whom he is very close – before finally arriving at the topic of the Olympics. Messi speaks openly. He wants to go to Beijing. He doesn't think that missing Barça's Champions League qualifier will be too much of a strain on the team (the first leg is on 12 or 13 August, the return leg is on the 26th or 27th, against an unknown team). On the contrary he maintains that 'Barcelona do not depend solely on me to win matches. They want to form a team that aspires to winning all the titles, if a player is absent on one particular day I don't think anything will come of it.' He is convinced that the club as much as the Barça fans will understand his decision.

He is wrong. Very wrong. It is immediately apparent upon hearing the comments from those in the room. While the journalists who have come from Buenos Aires might be satisfied with the position Leo has taken, happy that he has announced his Olympic dream and reaffirmed his desire to go for gold with the Albiceleste, the Catalan reporters are annoyed. They are coming off the back of two bad seasons for the club. The titles have vanished into oblivion one by one; the team that once dazzled the world has disappeared among dressing-room disputes and diatribes; its stars have been extinguished, and others, like Ronaldinho, have not made the headlines for months; Frank Rijkaard, the coach who directed the show for five years, has been dismissed; they have announced the departure of the superstars who led the Blaugrana to victory in the Champions League and La Liga; in summary, Barça – as a club and as a team – is going through a critical stage of much instability. At a time like this, it is difficult to digest Leo's decision. 'But how ... can Barcelona play the Champions League qualifiers with him not there? Who is paying him, Barça or Argentina?' And they dredge up the topic of the possible 8-million-euros-a-season 'megacontract', which Messi is to sign. And there's more: 'Messi is the player around whom the Blaugrana want to reconstruct a winning team, and he says "ciao" and he goes off to China. And if he gets injured, as has happened to him twice in this championship, who will pay?'

All this, and more, can be heard in the hallways of the Hesperia hotel. Few can stand the idea that the future Barça number 10 (everyone reckons he will inherit Ronaldinho's shirt number), the player who was so needed during long weeks of misfortune, can abandon them in this way.

The following day, in the Catalan sports papers, the headlines about Leo's declarations are mounting up. But they seem to understand the Flea's position. In keeping with their journalistic duty, many of them recall the regulations. 'In Messi's case, it is not possible for Barça to refuse because he is less than 23 years old,' writes *Sport*.

In the offices of the Nou Camp they do not get the message. They have no intention of losing Leo during the Champions League qualifiers. They immediately consult the guidelines to see if there is any possibility of not conceding to the Argentine team. Leo's father Jorge Messi, who meets with Barça technical secretary Txiki Begiristain a few days later, announces: 'Leo will do whatever he is obliged to do, to avoid being penalised by either party.' In other words, the decision to go to the Games does not depend solely on his son. If the Catalan club finds a way to prevent him, Lionel will have to resign himself to the fact and kiss his Olympic dream goodbye.

This is just the beginning of a tug-of-war between the AFA and Barcelona, which will go on for more than two months. In the meantime, having played the friendly against Catalunya (a match won by Pocho Lavezzi with one of his usual goals), Leo leaves for Argentina in a hurry. Coco Basile and the national team await him. The programme includes a mini tour of America and two qualifying matches for the 2010 World Cup. First, an important victory over Mexico; then a goalless draw against the United States at the New Jersey Giants' stadium. And then come the matches that matter: against Ecuador at the Monumental stadium and against Brazil at Belo Horizonte's Mieirão. The Albiceleste do not shine: two hard-earned draws.

Messi's commitments with the national team have finished; it is holiday time, time for advertising promotions and matches like the one he arranged with Ronaldinho on 28 June at the Monumental de Maturín in Venezuela, the second instalment of a charity match between Messi's friends and Ronnie's friends. A 7-7 result and a farewell to them being team-mates.

It is 2 July. Sergio Batista announces the list of the eighteen players who make up the national squad for the Olympics. Leo Messi is on it. It could be an end to the dispute. Julio Grondona, president of the AFA, also wants him there. 'Argentina will call up Messi in accordance with FIFA regulation, which states that he has to be with his national team at the Olympic Games. If I don't have Messi I don't have a team, and if he doesn't come and play with us, it will spark a precedent which will prompt other teams to ask for their players and we don't want that to happen either. It is logical for him to play for Argentina, since Barcelona have him for the whole year. There are very few competitions in which Messi can play with his country.'

Sounds straightforward, doesn't it? But Barcelona have no intention of waving the white flag. 'We have read up on it, we have attended meetings with the AFA and, ultimately, the regulations will be adhered to. If the regulations favour us, Messi will play in the Champions League qualifier,' maintains Begiristain.

On 15 July, Barcelona is back in session, with Pep Guardiola and without Ronaldinho. The Brazilian only has to complete his medical before he can play for Milan. It is a transfer which allows him to go to the Olympic Games. Barça had refused, since Ronnie is over 23 and FIFA does not oblige clubs to relinquish players older than 23. But Berlusconi's club will relinquish him. 'He's so lucky,' Leo must be thinking, not knowing what fate has in store for him. 'The club will not talk to him about the matter, it's a negotiation between Barcelona and the AFA,' says his mother, Celia. 'And Leo won't speak, he won't ask. He just waits for their answer.' And for the moment he goes to St Andrews, Scotland, where Barcelona's pre-season begins. It is 21 July. Two days later, Leo should be in Tokyo with the Olympic squad: a friendly against Japan is scheduled for 29 July. But Barça have not agreed. They have proposed to the Argentine Federation that they will relinquish the player after the American tour and after the first leg of the Champions League qualifier. If the result is good and favourable, of course. Messi would miss the first three matches of the Olympic qualifying stages, but as long as Argentina qualify, he could be there for the quarter-finals. It is a proposition that the AFA does not want to consider. The most they will accept is that Leo will take part in the

Barça pre-season, and then join the national team before the first match. They will not entertain the possibility that Messi won't go to the Games. They think that Barça will not want to come up against them, FIFA and, above all, the player, who has always expressed his desire to participate in the Olympics.

On 23 July, Joseph Blatter makes his contribution to the drama. 'The relinquishing of players under 23 has always been compulsory for all clubs. This same principle applies for Beijing 2008,' says the FIFA president, adding: 'Obstructing the participation of players under 23 years of age in the final phase of the tournament could be interpreted as an attack on the spirit of the Olympics.' But this still is not the final word, since the PFL can refute this argument. 'There is no legal obligation to relinquish footballers. In contrast to the female football tournament, the male Olympic football tournament is not included in the international calendar of matches approved by FIFA for the 2008–14 period.'

The only one who suffers from this push and pull is Lionel. He is nervous and acts 'a little strangely', according to his team-mates. So much so that after a forceful tackle during a practice in Scotland, he ends up in an altercation with Rafa Márquez. Pep Guardiola has to intervene to calm the excitement and ask a bad-tempered Leo to end things once and for all. It is a minor incident, it's silly; nonetheless it affects the new Barça coach. Guardiola takes the boy to one side. He talks to him, he wants to know what's going on, why the bad mood, why he's unhappy. He doesn't want to see him like this. He wants him to be happy playing football with Barça. A few words are enough to make Leo confess. He says, loud and clear, that he wants to go to Beijing. Guardiola promises to do everything possible. And he starts to take a stand after the first friendly against Hibernian

(6-0 to Barça with a great goal from the Flea). 'In the end,' declares Guardiola, 'Leo is the one who is worst affected in this story. There are only two or three weeks to go, some are saying one thing and others are saying something else. Blatter will have to sit down and look at the regulations and decide if he's staying with us or going to the Games.' Despite the demands, FIFA's decision takes another six days. In the interim comes Barça's second friendly against Dundee United, with three Messi goals, as well as words from Joan Laporta, the Barça club president, who restates the club's position, the consensus solution offered to the AFA, and announces that in the event of a negative verdict from FIFA, Barcelona will 'turn to the legal guidance of the CAS (Court of Arbitration for Sport) so that our claims are taken into account'.

In short the tug-of-war continues. There is less than a week remaining until Argentina's debut at the Games and no one knows if Leo will be there. On the websites of the Spanish and Argentine newspapers, the polls appear in abundance: 'Should the national team keep waiting for Messi?' asks *Clarín* of its readers. Evidently tired of this soap opera, they respond with a resounding 'no': 70 per cent, against 29 per cent who are willing to continue waiting.

'What should Barça do about Messi? Should they let him compete in the Olympics, or try to keep him for the Champions League qualifier?' replies *El País* from across the pond a few days later. Seventy-three per cent think Messi should participate in the Olympics.

On Tuesday 30 July Leo's first words are heard. His total silence has generated all different types of response. Gabriel Batistuta, for example, defends him. 'He is doing the right thing by not saying anything, because after the Olympics he is going to go back to playing with Barcelona and the national team.' Maradona, on the other hand, attacks him.

'He has to decide for himself. This is the moment to be more of a man. It is a great opportunity to grow. Either way, Barcelona will wait for him. That's why they gave him the number 10 shirt: because they want him. If they gave it to him, it's not because Messi is a movie star, it's because he is a phenomenon, a great player.' And, on the other hand, there is his family, who do not know which path to take. Jorge Messi confirms it: 'There is a conflict of interest here in which the player is being put in the middle. And they are using my son as cannon fodder. You can't generate prejudice towards a 21-year-old footballer, you never know how it will end. It's crazy that the player should have to make the decision. It can't be the case that those who are in charge of managing the football cannot reach an agreement. We don't know what to do.'

Finally, before travelling to Florence, where the team are playing a friendly against the Purples (Fiorentina), Leo speaks his mind and says what he proposes to do. 'If FIFA says I don't have to go, I'm not going; if I have to go, I'll go, without waiting for the CAS, because if I wait for the CAS it will already be too late for my team-mates and the national selection staff.'

And a few hours later, FIFA says that Messi should go to the Games. 'The sole judge of the Comisión del Estatuto del Jugador, Slim Aloulou (Túnez), has ruled that the relinquishing of players under 23 for the Beijing 2008 male Olympic football tournament is compulsory,' announces the statement from Zurich.

The news is received with great relief from the Argentine camp. 'Luckily, after a lot of going backwards and forwards, it was resolved in our favour,' confesses Sergio Batista.

After the match against Fiorentina (3-1 to Barça), Pep Guardiola comments: 'We will survive without Messi. However, I have a feeling that we are a little bit stronger with Messi. If he does not eventually return, we will ensure the team qualifies for the Champions League. And if he does return, we will welcome him back with open arms.'

There is a somewhat different response from the Blaugrana directors, whose opinion has not altered and who submit an appeal to the CAS. But in the meantime, instead of leaving for the American tour, Leo is off to China, promising to return if the CAS rule in favour of Barça.

In Shanghai, where he arrives on 1 August, Leo seems to recover the calm he had lost. He is laughing, and he finally seems happy during practice. He shares a room with Kun Agüero, as he did in the 2005 Under 20 World Cup. Thousands of PlayStation games, and *cumbia* music at full volume. The two get on well, they are relaxed, they let their hair down and do whatever they feel like. Checho breathes easily. The first time he saw Leo was at Barcelona, in the match against Catalunya. There were not many practices, and few with his team-mates, but fortunately he now has the chance to build up the group. For a while now, Batista has been thinking about where to position him on the field. 'I want Messi to come into the centre more, not be pinned to the touchline the way he is with Barcelona. I want him to generate more play, in front of Riquelme and behind Agüero,' he explains. Meanwhile, the Flea tells the press his dreams. 'For me, and for all the players, it would be really special to reclaim the title. We came here to win the gold medal. We'll take it slow and hopefully we can get it.' He denies that there is any problem between him and Riquelme (just before the World Cup qualifier against Brazil there had been rumours circulating of a dispute between the national number 10 and Messi). He maintains, although few believe him, that the relationship with Román has always been good. Regarding the controversy that kept him away from the national team, he explains: 'Batista understood me and so did my team-mates, they had no problem waiting for me. I did what I had to do. I hope that this situation will not be an issue any longer.' And it won't.

On 6 August, on the eve of Argentina-Ivory Coast, the first group A match, the CAS rules in favour of Barcelona. 'The Olympic tournament does not appear on FIFA's official calendar, and there is no decision from the FIFA executive committee which establishes an obligation to make players less than 23 years of age available to their countries for this championship,' explains the tribunal's ruling. However, it then requests that the parties concerned find 'a reasonable solution with respect to the players who wish to represent their countries at the Olympic Games'. And how do the parties react? Grondona is the first to make himself heard: 'Messi is not going anywhere.' Sergio Batista confirms: 'He will be on the pitch tomorrow.' And Leo? He makes no statements about the ruling and it seems that, though he may have been willing to return to Barça, he has no intention of returning to the fold now.

'He has told me that he wants to stay with the squad and he asks Barcelona to be considerate of his position,' assures Checho. Begiristain does not seem to be considerate: 'It is our wish – with our fans in mind – that Leo Messi be with the club,' he says. Satisfied with Barcelona's legal victory, Laporta orders the player's immediate return. But first, Guardiola wants to speak to Leo. 'I want to listen to him, and we will make a decision,' he says, 'but I can't relay it without having heard from the player.' Then there is a long, intercontinental phone conference between New York (where Barça are concluding their American tour against the Red Bulls) and Shanghai. Leo Messi asks Guardiola – who, after Barcelona '92, knows what it means to win an Olympic gold – to help him: he wants to stay in China and participate in the Games. Pep promises to find a solution. No sooner said than done. At the meeting, which takes place in a suite at the Saint Regis hotel, on the corner of Fifth Avenue and 53rd Street, he convinces Laporta and Begiristain. Messi is to stay in Beijing. But not without a few conditions. The first is that the AFA will take responsibility for medical insurance in case Messi is injured. The same clause that was demanded by Schalke 04 and Werder Bremen for Rafinha and Diego, the two Brazilians who were in the middle of a similar dispute between the clubs and the Brazilian Federation. The second is a 'personal agreement with Julio Grondona that the player will be relinquished from all the season's friendlies'. Guardiola is the one who announces Barcelona's decision to Leo. He calls him from the plane a few minutes before takeoff from New York. 'You're staying. Enjoy it,' he says.

On 7 August the Blaugrana expedition is on its way back to Barcelona. It falls to Begiristain and Guardiola to make the official announcement regarding the resolution of Messi's case. 'He found himself in a difficult position and he himself had expressed a desire to be with us for the pre-season,' explains the coach. 'But when he arrived in Beijing, he asked me personally not to request his return to Barcelona. I noted a lot of emotional tension. He has suffered brutal pressure, as has his family. I saw that he seemed very uncomfortable with the situation, and it also was not a good idea to bring him here if his head was in Beijing. Now, after this whole drama, the best thing is for him to play, to enjoy it, to be happy and for him to return content. The Barça fan-base knows that we have an extraordinary player and that he will do wonderful things when he returns. The people will be understanding towards him.'

Messi goes onto the pitch to face the Ivory Coast wearing the Argentine number 15 shirt. And he demonstrates why his presence at the Olympic Games was so important. Towards the end of the first half, he receives a 45-yard pass from Riquelme, he picks up the pace and, almost from the penalty spot, places it delicately into the net. Five minutes from the final whistle, when the scoreboard seems stuck at 1-1 (Cissé responded to Leo's goal), the Flea takes a quick free kick with Román on the edge of the area and it takes a wicked deflection. The Elephants' goalie makes the save and Lautaro Acosta – who secured the team's qualification for the Games – then finds it easy to score the final goal to make it 2-1.

A few seconds from the end, Batista substitutes Leo and in doing so gives him the opportunity to be applauded by the Chinese crowd. They did it throughout the match and, when his picture appeared on the Olympic stadium screen, regardless of the fact that the Argentine national anthem was playing, a chant of 'Messi, Messi' began to pick up in the stands. He is one of the best-known sportsmen in the People's Republic of China. He sells well, from shirts to Pepsi Cola, and the children want to be like him. For the moment, let's leave aside his popularity, which grew exponentially during the Olympics, to the point that he joined FIFA's ranks as one of the best-known sportsmen, and at the end of the tournament will be chosen by the online users of MyBestPlay as the most favoured footballer of the Olympics, alongside athletes such as Michael Phelps, the swim king, or Usain Bolt, the fastest man in the world. Let's return to the match. Beneath the question of favourite footballers, which dominates the conversation, there is also a sense of happiness at the resolution of the conflict. This time it is Leo's turn to speak, and to thank Guardiola. 'He was a player and he knows how a player feels at those moments,' he says. 'He knew that I was in a situation that was difficult for me and he has supported me ever since he arrived at Barcelona, since the first day when I spoke to him. He has been outstanding, and the truth is that I am very grateful.' With the chapter

closed once and for all, his thoughts now turn to his friend
Ronaldinho's Brazil, the other favourite to win the title: 'If
we reach a final against Brazil, it will be much more difficult
because Ronnie will be there. It is always great to win a final,
and even more so against Brazil,' jokes the Flea, but before
that, there is 'Australia, tough competitors, strong, who play
well in the air and who will create a tricky match. It's going
to be extremely difficult.'

It certainly is. Fifteen minutes from the end, the score at
the Shanghai Olympic stadium still stands at 0-0. Argentina,
at least in the first half, play better than in the debut match,
they create chances, but Federici, the Australian goalkeeper,
is difficult to beat. Then, in a few seconds, after various
touches between Riquelme and Messi, Román plays the ball
out to the left to Di María, who crosses into the centre and
Pocho Lavezzi converts it. It's the victory goal.

On the other side of the world, two days after 12 August, a
Messi-less Barcelona also win: 4-0 against Wisła Cracovia in the
first leg of the preliminary round of the Champions League.
The Blaugrana fears vanish. But let's go back to China. With
their pass to the quarter-finals in the bag, the Albiceleste relo-
cate to the Olympic Village in Beijing. Nothing fancy for the
spoiled footballers, but lots of encounters. 'We were eating,'
recalls Oscar Ustari, 'and we saw him arrive, queue for his
food and sit down at the table. "Hi, I'm Kobe" (Bryant), he
said to us. He spoke to us in Spanish, looked for Messi, and
chatted to him for a bit. And we took the opportunity of taking a few photos. When it came to saying goodbye, he made
the gesture of taking off his hat, looked directly at Leo, and
said to him: "Messi, you're the best." We were in awe. Nadal
(Rafa) also came over. When you're with Leo, you can't just
cruise along, they stop you everywhere you go.'

But there are not only encounters with celebrities from
all over the world. In Beijing they also have to face Serbia.

Checho rests Leo, keeps the already-cautioned Riquelme and Agüero on the bench, and lets the subs play. Seven changes, an overhaul which nonetheless leads to victory. 2-0 (a Lavezzi penalty and a Buonanotte free kick); nine consecutive Olympic victories (beating the record held by Uruguay for 80 years); first place in the group. The only ones who lost out were the 60,000 spectators who rushed to the Beijing Workers' Stadium to see Messi in action. During the first half they chant his name and when, at the end of the match, they see that the Flea is not coming on, they begin to whistle at the Argentine team. In the end, the coach has to justify himself. 'The people of China have to understand that we came here with an objective, that of winning the gold medal. It wasn't only Messi who didn't play today. Riquelme, Agüero and Garay didn't play either. I was thinking of the best for Argentina. If they were annoyed, it's bad luck. I hope they forgive me.'

The next fixture, also at the Beijing Workers' Stadium, is against Holland on 16 August. Maradona is also in the stands, to cheer for the national team, and for Kun, who is the boyfriend of his daughter Giannina. There is no room for mistakes. Leo knows it and puts on a show. Here is how *Clarín* describes it: 'How many wishes will be granted by this genie, who appears during the national team matches? If there were three in the original story, perhaps Batista's team will be left short of what they need from this magical figure who arrived from Barcelona and who did very well again today, with a fantastic goal and an incredible pass – to resolve a story that had become difficult and in which Holland was very close to stealing the dream of reclaiming the Olympic gold.' But what did the Flea do this time? He settled an extremely complicated match. How? Dodging around one defender, dummying the goalie to leave him in the dust, and blasting it into the net before any desperate

Dutchmen had the chance to intervene. 1-0. Then, in the fourteenth minute of extra time, he invents perfect geometry so that Di María can predict the course of a strong shot, a low cross, which secures the 2-1. And Argentina are to face Brazil in the semi-finals.

The *Clásico par excellence*, the anticipated final, the perfect occasion to avenge the most recent historic encounters (the defeats in the finals of the 2004 Copa América in Peru, in the 2005 Copa Confederaciones and again in the 2007 Copa América in Venezuela). The Olympic champions Argentina, against Brazil, who have never won the gold; it is the match that Leo dreamt of, although one stage higher in the competition. And as if that weren't enough, there is the duel between Leo and Ronaldinho: two friends, two ex-team-mates, the talented youngster against the former Ballon d'Or winner, the present against the past, the current star against the champion who is looking to be reborn from the ashes. The list could go on and on. The debate over who is greater is wide open. Everyone has their own opinion. Even Kun gets involved: 'Lionel, nowadays, is better than Ronaldinho. He's the best player in the world.'

Messi avoids the topic, but he does not shy away from the avalanche of questions: 'I'm not one to make predictions, but Ronnie: remember the gold belongs to Argentina! My dream is the dream of the whole Argentine team. And more so now, for Ustari, for my friend [Oscar has been injured in the match against Holland and cannot keep goal for the Albiceleste]. It will be hard,' he says, 'it is always difficult against Brazil. We are both extremely worn out from the extra time in our quarter-finals matches. Brazil has an incredible team, but our team is immense. We are playing for the same thing, to see who gets the gold, and they won the last final we played. I'm still cross about the final of the Copa América. Now it's our turn ...' And indeed it is Argentina's turn, but in a way no one had imagined. They quash, humiliate and make fun of Brazil. Agüero, with two goals and a hand in the third (he is fouled and Riquelme converts the penalty), and his celebrations – where he mimes putting a dummy in his mouth (Giannina is expecting a baby) – are all evidence of the weakness of Dunga's team and Ronaldinho's decline. 'Nowadays,' writes *El País*, 'the Brazilian is a false player, more given to pulling faces, cheerful chatter and other similar gestures, which are only an attempt to win front pages and the applause of a Chinese crowd who are novices when it comes to football. As much as he disguises his decline with lots of theatricality, the football he has left in him does not guarantee him a performance, except for the ball being as dead as he is: he still manages to take free kicks.' A cruel portrait of someone who was once the world number one. But even more cruel is the photo that appears in the media across the world the following day: Ronnie in his yellow number 10 shirt and captain's armband, finding solace, head bowed, in the arms of his 'little brother' Messi. Lionel is standing on tiptoes in order to console his idol. There is a lot of affection in that picture, but there is also a lot of melancholy. Without making a big impression, Leo has won that highly anticipated duel. He is happy. Ronnie only wants to hide, to disappear from the face of the earth. 'I'm sad, very sad,' he will say later. For him, this was the opportunity to be seen again in the world. He has failed. Leo, on the other hand, is making his way towards gold.

At twelve o'clock on Saturday 23 August (one in the morning in Argentina) at the National Stadium, nicknamed the Bird's Nest, the final of the Olympic Games football tournament begins. Opponent: Nigeria – just like in Atlanta '96 and in the 2005 Under 20 World Cup in Holland. In the American Olympics, Nwankwo Kanu's Nigeria took home the gold after a 3-2 final, considered by FIFA to be one of the ten most memorable matches in a century of Olympic football. Argentine revenge comes in 2005, in Holland. And the protagonist, the one who defeats the Green Eagles, is Lionel: two penalties. Fifteen players from that final (including Messi and Kun) find themselves at the ground in Beijing. 'We're going to win, I have no doubt about it. 2-0 would be perfect,' prophesies Diego Maradona. It is not that easy.

The heat is so oppressive that after 30 minutes of the first half, Hungarian referee Victor Kassai calls a basketball-style timeout so the teams can cool down. A break that is repeated in the second half. The pitch is hard, dry and the Green Eagles leave no spaces uncovered. Messi and Agüero are alone up front. Their tiny runs with touches and dodges make no impression on the giant Nigerians. Riquelme is not having a good day. Midfielders Gago and 'Chief' Mascherano are working hard. The match is bad, wretched, boring, tiring. Until the 57th minute: there is a scuffle between an Argentine and an African, the ball rebounds towards the centre of the pitch, Messi recovers it, turns, and passes it perfectly, out deep, to Ángel Di María. The ex-Rosario Central midfielder for Benfica, the sensation of the Games, gallops away freely on the left. And on the edge of the area, in front of Vanzekin who desperately comes off his line, he is inspired to lift the ball softly with his left foot and send it lightly through the heavy Beijing air. The Nigerian goalkeeper can do nothing but get up and, motionless in the penalty area, watch from afar as the ball bounces into the net – a work of art that deserves the gold. Argentina return to the top after four years on the highest step of the podium at Athens. Messi, with his arms around Kun, celebrates the fulfilment of the dream. He has triumphed over all the legal objections, over all those who didn't want to let him experience this fairytale. And he says it out loud: 'After everything that was said and discussed, it was worth coming.'

Chapter 35

Happiness

27 May 2009

Between Lexington Avenue and Fifth Avenue, Pakistani cab driver Happy Cabby offers customers his life philosophy: 'To make others happy, you must be happy yourself. That is where happiness lies,' he says, turning in his seat to face the passengers and tapping his head with his index finger. 'Yes, it all depends on you to make other people and the world happy.' Perhaps Leo has also felt this good news, conveyed over the noise of Midtown; one thing for sure is that the happiest year of his life began precisely here, in New York, on the corner of Fifth Avenue and 53rd Street, in the Saint Regis hotel suite, when Pep Guardiola convinced Laporta and Begiristain to let Messi stay in Beijing. Permission to participate in the Olympic Games has been without a doubt the biggest motivation for the Argentine and has created a special relationship between the Flea and the Blaugrana coach.

'Everything began over there in Beijing, with the gold medal. He has been happier than ever before,' says his father, Jorge. 'Yes, that's what Pep wanted, for him to get his dream.' 'I don't know ... to me he seems very happy – I think we succeeded,' admits Guardiola. Indeed, the young manager was conscious of the fact that the key to the Flea being able to make the Barcelona camp happy was first to make him happy. And he has managed it. Txiki Begiristain, sporting director of Barça, confirms it: 'If, when he sees you, he jokes with you, then he's happy, if he doesn't seem to see you and looks the other way, something's wrong. Leo has spent the whole year joking with me and with whomever he comes across.' And his team-mates say the same. 'He can only play his best football when he's happy and comfortable,' says Xavi. 'He has been happy,' adds Puyol, the captain, 'but I have also seen him angry. You have no idea what he's like when he doesn't win!' But this has not happened during the 2008–09 season, since Barcelona have won everything: La Liga, the Copa del Rey and the Champions League, the first Spanish team to win the triple and a feat accomplished by only five European clubs (the last to do so was Manchester United ten years earlier). In addition, they have won the Spanish Super Cup and the European Super Cup. Leo has scored more goals than ever before in his professional career. Twenty-three in La Liga, the fourth-highest scorer after Diego Forlán, Samuel Eto'o and David Villa. And let's not forget the 5,000th goal in the Catalan club's Liga history, which Leo scores on 1 February 2009 in Santander against Racing. His second of the match, which secures a victory for Barça. Next up: six more in the Copa del Rey, the tournament's top goal scorer, and he only played 452 minutes (an average of a goal every 75 minutes), and two in the Spanish Super Cup. And nine goals in the Champions League, highest goal scorer in the European tournament. In contrast to the previous two years, he did not sustain even a minor injury in all his 51 matches. In addition to all that he garnered individual recognition. The Spanish coaches voted him the best Liga foreigner, over Forlán, Dani Alves and Kanouté, and according to the club coaches who reached the previous season's Champions League final sixteen, he was the best footballer and best forward of the continental tournament, beating Cristiano

Ronaldo to the punch. It's true that the team's (spectacular) performance has helped him to win these trophies, but ever since he put on the number 10 shirt, Messi has taken a step forward, he has taken up the mantle in the dressing room and on the pitch, he has given it his all, and done it all in an unassuming manner. 'Ever since I met him, at fourteen,' declares Blaugrana defender Gerard Piqué, 'he has always been the same. He has never thought of himself as the best, but he has always known that we all consider him the best.'

At the Grimaldi Forum in Monte Carlo – dressed elegantly in a dark suit, matching tie and white shirt – after having received the honour of best 2008–09 Champions League player, Leo comments: 'It has been an incredible year. I have thoroughly enjoyed it.' And to those who ask him what has been the most magical moment, he responds: 'There were so many wonderful moments that it would be impossible to pick one.'

Seeing as the champion does not know how to choose between so many happy occasions, we will give it a try.

27 May 2009, Olympic Stadium, Rome. Champions League final: Barcelona-Manchester United

Although Messi has one European Cup to his name, it has never felt like his. Because he was not there on the pitch on the evening of 17 May 2006 at the Saint-Denis stadium in Paris. The Flea was not granted permission to play by the medics, despite having repeated over and over that he was fine, that his thigh injury did not hurt any more. He watched the final, against Thierry Henry's Arsenal, from the stands. And during the moments of joy, the hugs and the celebrations, he shut himself into the dressing room in a huff. His friends Deco and Ronaldinho were the ones who got him out of there and tried to make him see that the victory belonged to him as well. Without much success, because to him you have to play in order to feel like a champion.

This time it is different. Leo knows it and feels it. He has been a decisive contributing factor in bringing Barcelona to Rome. With eight goals which make him the tournament's top goal scorer, ahead of Henry who has five and Berbatov, Rooney and Cristiano Ronaldo who have four apiece. Messi scores five goals in the group phase: two against Shakhtar Donetsk in Ukraine, to regain a match which had been an uphill struggle for the Blaugrana; another two against FC Basel: one in Switzerland, which ended up being a Barcelona attack-fest (0-5), and the other at the Nou Camp. The final one is against Sporting Lisbon. The Portuguese team suffered at the hands of Barça's goal-scoring ability when they were dealt a 2-5 blow on their home turf. And in the knockout rounds Lionel adds another three, all in front of the home crowd at the Nou Camp: one against Olympique Lyonnais in the quarter-final and two against Bayern Munich, among which he displays without a doubt his best football of the whole season. The Flea does not score in the semi-final against Chelsea. The Blaugrana hero is Andrés Iniesta with his heavenly shot in the 93rd minute, but it was Leo Messi who supplied the ball to the Blaugrana number 8 in the 'D'. At long last ... after working day and night, the Barça number 10 has earned the right to be a team leader. The final pits the Liga champions and the 2008–09 Premier League champions against each other – two teams full of great players. Here are the teamsheets. Barcelona: Valdés, Puyol, Touré, Piqué, Sylvinho, Busquets, Xavi, Iniesta, Messi, Henry, Eto'o. Manchester United: Van Der Sar, O'Shea, Vidic, Ferdinand, Evra, Park, Anderson, Carrick, Rooney, Giggs, Cristiano Ronaldo.

Sir Alex Ferguson faces the final with his infinite experience, and Pep Guardiola, as the new sensation of the season.

It is a match European football fans could only dream of, the best fixture possible, between two teams that put on the best show out of anyone on the continent. And, as Leo declares, it is 'the most important game of my career'. He says it just before catching his flight to Rome. It is his first time in the Eternal City, but he doesn't like sightseeing – he is only going to the Italian capital to win. Although he says that 'they are the title holders, so if there is a favourite in a match like this – which there isn't always – then they are the favourites on this occasion'.

The media is promoting the match as the great duel between Cristiano Ronaldo and Leo Messi. They show each player's Champions League statistics and maintain that they are playing for the Ballon d'Or in Rome. It is a chance for the Flea to overtake a rival who beat him by 165 points in *France Football*'s Ballon d'Or vote on 2 December 2008, and who confirmed his place at the top by winning FIFA World Player of the Year on 12 January 2009. But Lionel doesn't see it that way. 'It would be reductive and disrespectful to two great teams, who are currently playing the best football. Two teams who have many other players who can be decisive.' In other words, there is no personal contest with Cristiano to see who is better. 'I am sure he thinks the same as I do: the important thing is the prize at stake for the team. One thing for sure is that whoever wins in Rome will be heralded as the best team in Europe.'

All true, but the two know that they are being watched by half the world. Cristiano Ronaldo, who, despite not having had a wonderful season, is longing to show that he is still number one, is really buzzing at the start of the match. In the first minute he takes a free kick from 35 yards. Five steps back as usual, rocking on his left leg, and the Portuguese shoots. A great shot. The ball spins, hitting Víctor Valdés on the chest, and he's unable to control it. In a final attempt to salvage the situation, Piqué anticipates the Korean Ji-Sun Park at the corner flag. Cristiano puts his head in his hands. Before Messi has touched the ball, the white-shirted number 7 has given quite a performance: three shots and a yellow card for Piqué, who had tried to stop him with an obstructive foul. Manchester United's best play is coming from Cristiano's boots. In contrast, Lionel has yet to enter the game. His father, Jorge, sees it too: 'I saw that Leo was out of the game for quite a while, and only once we scored the goal I began to see him get more involved.' In fact, the Flea does not make an appearance until nine minutes after Eto'o has put Barcelona in front. He leaves the right-hand touchline, looks to move into the centre, and unleashes a cracking shot from 35 yards – gliding low just above the ground. Messi is playing as a dummy centre forward to force the Manchester United central defenders out of position – something Ferguson would later say 'surprised us and made it difficult for us to mark him'. It seems to be true, because every time the Argentine has the ball between his feet, he causes problems for the English team's defence. Barça begin to take control of the game and although it is not his best night and he only manages to infiltrate the forest of white shirts a few times, Messi is getting better and better. Manchester United's French left back, Patrice Evra – the man who won them the duel with Lionel in April 2008 (0-0 in the first leg, 1-0 in the return leg) – had already predicted it: 'Messi is "hungrier" and he is a better player now than he was a year ago.' He is right: 84 per cent of Leo's passes are on target. His angles are close to perfection, so much so that a veteran like Ryan Giggs says: 'When you see how they move you can't help but be amazed.' Then comes the 70th minute, when the Flea ascends to the Roman heavens. The smallest (it is worth noting that he is 1.69m) becomes the greatest.

The action: Xavi recovers the ball after a short rebound from the English defence, he heads towards the box, lifts his head and sends in a cross with spin – smooth and precise. With his back to the defenders, Messi goes up for it, very high, and heads the ball in at the opposite post from where the goalie is. It's 2-0.

The explanation: 'When Xavi got the ball I got in position because I thought he would pass it there: I saw that Van Der Sar was a little off his line and I headed it.'

The photo: Messi suspended in the air, immobile, high, very high, leaning back. The ball, travelling on its arc, seems like it's going over the bar. In front, Van Der Sar, in yellow, watches it, open-mouthed, with a look of terror on his face. Close, very close, although out of focus, Rio Ferdinand, twenty centimetres taller than the Argentine, could do nothing to prevent that jump.

The precedent: Many people were betting on the number 10 scoring for Barça in the final. The bookies were offering very short odds. But few would have predicted a header. Up until that point he had only scored two. Pep Guardiola – who psyched up his players before the final by showing a clip from Ridley Scott's *Gladiator* – had been the only one to prophesy it. At a press conference in Santander on 1 February 2009, the day before the match against Racing, when asked if Messi needed to score more headers in order to become the best player in the world, the coach from Santpedor replied: 'I advise you not to test him because one day he'll score an incredible header and shut you all up.'

The curiosity: 'I didn't see my son's goal,' admits Jorge Messi, in the stands with his wife Celia, Leo's siblings and their respective families. 'At that moment I looked down, I don't know if it was due to nerves. I saw it afterwards on TV and I had honestly never seen him jump so high. But when did he take off his boot?' Because no sooner has his son come back down to earth – and before being inundated with hugs from his team-mates – than he does a lap holding up his new blue boot, as homage to Argentina. Meanwhile, the 20,000 Barça fans in the Olympic stadium chant his name. At the end of the match, he is the first to be hugged by Guardiola – the man who has been so good to him. And what of the other competitor in the duel? Cristiano Ronaldo? He finishes the match powerless and wound up, he argues with Rooney, and receives a yellow card for a pointless foul on Puyol. Later, hurt, and already in his suit, he says: 'It wasn't a match between Messi and me, but his team was better than us, and he was too because he scored.'

The defeated pays homage to the victor. This time, Leo does feel that the cup is his. He kisses it, he hugs it, he adores it, he takes it on a lap around the ground, and he parties until three in the morning with his team-mates, friends and family. 'I feel like the happiest man in the world. It's like I'm dreaming, it's the most important victory of my life. I dedicate it to my family and to Argentina. This team deserves it after the great work they have put in all year,' declares Messi. Great work, and some marvellous football, exquisite, as recognised by the media across the world. But the front cover photos and the big headlines are reserved for the Flea. 'Messi, king of Europe,' runs the headline in *Corriere dello Sport*, the Rome sports paper; 'SuperMessi,' says the *Gazzetta dello Sport*; 'Messi and Barcelona on top of the world,' reads the headline in *La Nación* in Buenos Aires. Meanwhile, Buenos Aires sports paper *Olé* carries a picture of Leo with the cup, with the caption: 'Don't ask me to head it.' 'Marvellous Messi is too much for United,' reads the headline in *The Times*, which opts for the same photo as *El País*. A smiling Messi, pointing his fingers in the air, and a matter-of-fact headline: 'Messi is the best'. And no one argues.

2 May 2009, Bernabéu stadium, Madrid. The 34th match day
of La Liga: Real Madrid-Barcelona

There is no contest; no possible comparison can be made. Two completely distinct worlds. Two different ways of understanding football, but when they eventually come face to face, there is no league position that matters, and no run of winning results that counts. The cruel, numerical reality unfolds on the pitch at the Bernabéu: six goals against two – something that has never been seen before. The greatest humiliation in the Whites' history. The Blaugrana had never previously scored six goals at the Bernabéu; the result that came closest was 0-5 in 1974, when one Johan Cruyff played for Barça. And to think that before that sweltering Madrid night, Whites coach Juande Ramos and his boys thought they could win it. They were intending to close the gap, move within one point of Barcelona and joyfully sing their way through their last four Liga fixtures. Deep down they have reasons to be optimistic: they have come a long way since Barça beat them at the Nou Camp on 13 December 2008 (2-0, with goals from Eto'o and Leo, obviously), relegating them to twelve points. Despite an internal crisis which has affected the club, leading to Ramón Calderón's dismissal, the Whites have broken records: 52 points out of a possible 54, eighteen games without loss. In contrast to the Champions League (they were eliminated in the final sixteen 0-5 by Rafa Benítez's Liverpool), when it comes to La Liga they are still hopeful. True, this Barça team, together with Messi – who has already scored 21 goals in the championship – inspire fear. But when asked if he has thought about copying Chelsea manager Guus Hiddink's plan (implemented in the first leg of the Champions League semi-finals) the Real Madrid manager insists: 'I have no anti-Messi plan because taking him out doesn't guarantee anything. We have to try not to let Barcelona have a good day and work hard together as a team.' It is hard work that seems to bear fruit in the thirteenth minute, when Pipita Higuaín puts them ahead. But it's an illusion. The teams are worlds apart, because the men in red-and-blue shirts emanate football from every pore. They represent the beauty of the game in its purest form, the art of sophisticated play to the nth degree of potential. They play with ease, the passes are so precise and fluid it is as if they are in a training session. They ridicule the Whites. The white ball slides from side to side across the green carpet, bam, boom, until it finds someone who transforms it into an idea, into something magical, or simply into a chance at goal. Like Leo, for example, who lifts the ball lightly; it sails over Sergio Ramos, who tries desperately to reach it, and lands delicately at the feet of Henry, who puts it elegantly and efficiently past Casillas to finish. Good grief, where would Real Madrid be without 'Saint' Iker? The shots are coming from every angle and there are too many to count. It is a real nightmare for the Real goalie. Guardiola's men waste opportunities: out of selfishness, as is the case with Messi, who really wants to score against Madrid (in his previous three trips to the Bernabéu he has never once scored) and who fails to see his unmarked team-mate; or out of too much generosity, as is the case with Iniesta's yellow boots, which, after a duet of one-twos all the way up the pitch with the Argentine, do not seal the deal, and give the ball to the Flea who shoots at close range – blocked by Iker. But in any case, by the 45th minute there have already been three goals scored. After one from Henry, and one from Puyol, the captain, the half-time scoreboard is closed by Leo, who finally experiences the joy of scoring on the Whites' home turf. Xavi, the king of the night, steals the ball from Lass Diarrá in the middle. He offers it to Leo, who finishes it with a shot at the near post. The Bernabéu falls silent and the sandwich which is traditionally eaten in the break before kick-off tastes more bitter. The game recommences and it seems that Pep Guardiola's men do not want to be cruel to such renowned opponents. The Liga chasers bounce back momentarily when Sergio Ramos heads in a Robben free kick to close the gap. But it lasts for a matter of minutes. The Barça players control the game as they please. And the goals score themselves: because Xavi, the 'doctor', creates ever more beautiful assists; because Iniesta makes one dribbling run after another; because Henry makes a laughing stock of Ramos and scores his second goal; because Messi is like a spirit who appears on any part of the pitch, wherever you least expect him. Casillas is not expecting him either, and finds himself on his backside, while the ball slides into the net. That makes five, and the kid from Rosario can run towards the cameras, holding his blue-and-red shirt up between his teeth, showing the one beneath, which has a flower and the words 'Síndrome X Frágil'. For a while now, Leo has collaborated with the Catalan organisation that helps families who have children affected by fragile X chromosome syndrome (FXS) – also known as Martin-Bell syndrome. It is a genetic disorder passed down through families that can cause serious difficulties: from learning problems to diminished intellectual capacity. It affects one in every 4,000 boys and one in every 6,000 girls, and one in 250 women is a carrier without having any symptoms. It is not the first time that Messi is helping this organisation. In 2008 he was a patron of the book *39 historias solidarias alrededor del deporte* (*39 Stories of Solidarity in Sport*), written by Catalan journalists who donated the proceeds of its sale to the organisation. But this gesture of solidarity and this goal dedication is beamed around the world and tells millions of people about a genetic problem as yet under-researched. It is an example of how a ball in the back of the net can serve as something more than just a football result. But let's return to a game which has no precedent, because Barça do what they like. Gerard Piqué is a good example, he is majestic at the back – he doesn't make a single mistake – and up front he manages to score the sixth goal, the goal that brings sadness. Real Madrid's Liga career is over. And no one will knock Barcelona off the top spot, since they are now seven points clear. And perhaps no one would have knocked them off even if the result had been different. But this match serves as a reminder of the show put on by Leo Messi and Guardiola's Blaugrana team throughout the entire season, in Spain as well as in Europe. And it closes a dark chapter for Madrid: the Whites just have to wait for the elections, a new president, or better still, a saviour (Florentino Pérez), who, with a few million, will rebuild this weak team, who up until this point had been champions. But there is something more: the 2-6 scoreline also tastes of revenge. The last time Barça visited the Bernabéu, on 7 May 2008, the players stood in two lines to form a walkway onto the pitch in order to honour Real Madrid, who had recently been declared Liga champions. It was a morbid match. And it finished in a resounding 4-1 defeat – a double humiliation for the Catalans. 'Before the match,' declared Leo to the *Gazzetta dello Sport*, 'we said we weren't thinking about getting "revenge" for the walkway from the previous year, but evidently, deep down, there was still a thorn in our sides which bothered us. More because of the result and the way in which we had lost than because of the walkway ... We removed the thorn brilliantly.'

13 May 2009, Mestalla stadium, Valencia. Final of the Copa del Rey: Athletic Bilbao-Barcelona

'Messi is the king' proclaims a yellow placard, which is being waved in the curve of the stadium where the Barcelona fans are sitting. No offence intended to Juan Carlos, king of Spain, who is watching the match from the stands, but the Barça fans are right. In his first final since he joined the Blaugrana first team, Leo is crowned king of the pitch. He plays and he creates play, he scores and he creates goals. Nothing like Diego Armando Maradona did 25 years previously, on 5 May 1984, in the same final against Athletic. At the final whistle (the match had ended with the Bilbao Lions winning 1-0 thanks to a goal from Endico), Maradona aimed a kick at Sola and set off an impressive fight on the Bernabéu pitch. Practically all of the players were implicated in the battle. Maradona – who was appearing in his last fixture in a Barça shirt and was packing his bags for Napoli – wanted revenge over Athletic defender Andoni Goikoetxea, who had broken his leg nine months earlier. The result: an incredible punch-up and a three-month ban for six players. At that time the Golden Boy was 24, while the Flea is still only 21, but he seems more mature than Diego. He shows no sign of nerves and, together with Xavi, he is the central figure in the Blaugrana performance. He has a hand in three of Barcelona's four goals, which put paid to Athletic's dreams of winning their 24th cup. The Bilbaoans have the advantage, and they proudly resist until the second half when, just at the right moment, Messi appears. Leo makes a beautiful pass to Eto'o – the Cameroonian shoots hard across goal, Gorka Iraizoz responds, the ball rebounds freely. Keeping incredibly cool, the Barça number 10 goes for the shot and scores. It is 1-2 – the deciding goal of the match. The Flea's show continues: a perfect pass to Bojan, which he finishes like a pro to make it three. He also plays a part in the fourth: Leo provokes the foul, which Xavi converts with a fantastic free kick into the net. Then Messi looks for the pass that allows Eto'o to score – a reward for his self-denial throughout the entire match. And were it not for Gorka, who saves it with his foot, the Cameroonian almost would have made it. Barça win their 25th Copa del Rey. Mestalla is a scene of celebrations and Leo's name is the most chanted. And next day *Marca* writes: 'Messi hardly ever fails in this type of fixture, and yesterday he showed once again that he is the most decisive player of the Spanish Liga. The titles are beginning to rain down on this footballer who, without a doubt, will be the symbol of an era.'

23 August 2009, Nou Camp stadium, Barcelona. Return leg of the Spanish Super Cup: Barcelona-Athletic Bilbao

He didn't play in the first leg in San Mamés, but in the return leg, a week later, Lionel is on the pitch from the first minute onwards. Alongside him is the brand-new Blaugrana signing: Zlatan Ibrahimović, signed in exchange for 45 million euros and Samuel Eto'o's transfer to Inter. Without Leo, Ibrahimović and the injured Iniesta, Pep's team returned from Bilbao with a 1-2 result (goals from De Marcos, Xavi and Pedro) and the Super Cup almost in the bag. In reality it is a strange final, since Barça should have had to play against themselves, being both Liga and Copa del Rey champions, but the organisation has stipulated that they should face the Copa del Rey runners-up, Athletic Bilbao. It makes no difference, because in front of their fans, Barça are in fact playing Barça: although they are persistent and they put up a noble fight, the Athletic players are mere testimonial witnesses. The Flea is on hand again to make an impact and, as on other occasions, starts off slowly, but when he gets going he is lethal – when he passes as much as when he finishes. He starts off by wasting a face-to-face chance against Iraizoz, the Bilbaoan goalkeeper. He follows that up by setting up the new arrival (Ibrahimović) in a brilliant sequence, where the Argentine passes and the Swede controls it on his chest, before finishing it by shooting over the goalie. He sums it all up with a sensational move that breaks through the Lions' defence. Xavi

passes to Ibrahimović, the striker back-heels it to Messi, and
the Argentine dodges past the central defender with his left
foot, in order to bounce the ball into the goalmouth with his
right. He creates an impossible, fantastic goal – the goal of a
real superstar. It is the advantage that has been a while coming, because throughout the first half, Barça have not been
very precise when it comes to finishing. They had been lacking shots on target, but along comes Messi, who kick-starts
the party with his incredible goal and finishes it up from the
penalty spot in the 67th minute. After a confusing exchange
that results in a foul on Alves – according to the referee – Leo
places the ball on the spot and makes no mistake in getting
it in the back of the net, to the right of Gorka. The game is
already won, but before the festivities begin, Bojan is able to
add his goal to the celebrations. It is Barça's fourth consecutive title. And it's not over yet.

28 August 2009, Stade Louis II, Monaco. UEFA Super Cup: Barcelona-Shakhtar Donetsk

'Leo left it to me. The assist was practically a goal, I just had
to tap it in,' says Pedro Eliezer Rodríguez Ledesma, better
known as Pedrito. He is a 22-year-old Brazilian player, and
Barcelona's number 17. He arrived at Barcelona as a boy of
fifteen, and is one of eight called upon by Pep Guardiola
for the seemingly endless UEFA Super Cup match. The
eternal reserves player just signed his first professional contract with Barça on 20 August; he is the striker who won the
Champions League after only playing one minute of football and without even touching the ball. Well … in the 81st
minute Pedrito comes on for Zlatan Ibrahimović and in the
115th, after a back-and-forth with Messi, he finds the perfect
angle, the gap just by Pyatov's goalpost, in order to draw a
line under a gruelling match and win Barça their fifth cup
of the season. But in reality, and with great humility, the

little Brazilian recognises that the credit belongs to Messi. It has not been an easy match. The strategy designed by Mircea Lucescu, the sly dugout veteran, is working. The defence organised by the Romanian coach blocks successive attacks by Guardiola's men. They have to wait until half an hour into the game before seeing their first result. After a free kick, Leo, dribbling quickly and craftily, sees his shot blocked twice by the Ukrainian goalkeeper. But the Barça number 10 and his team-mates never tire of looking for the gaps, undeterred by the fact that Lucescu's men turn the counter-attack into their greatest weapon.

And here goes Leo Messi again, free kick just on the edge of the area. The ball is intercepted on its arc by the players in the wall. Leo and the other Blaugrana players protest. They demand a penalty. According to them, a defender has blocked the ball with his elbow. The first half ends and in the second half things are not much different. On the Stade Louis II pitch, in terrible conditions, the scoreline does not budge. The nerves are starting to show – so much so that after breaking away into the area only to end up in a tangle of opponents, Leo pushes a Shakhtar defender and finds himself head to head with Darijo Srna – an offence that earns him a caution.

There are five minutes of extra time remaining, five minutes until penalties, when Leo creates a brilliant pass to Pedrito. It is shot number 21 for Barça, and it is the victory shot. The Brazilian kicks it with his right while falling to the ground and sends this Barça team on their way to being legendary. It is the goal that brings Pep's team in line with Barça's five-cup team: the magnificent team made up of Ramallets, Martín, Biosca, Seguer, Gonzalvo III, Bosch, Basora, César, Vila, Kubala and Manchón. In the 1951–52 season, coach Ferdinand Daucik won La Liga, the Copa de España, the Copa Latina, the Copa Eva Duarte (named after Evita) and the Copa Martini & Rossi. It's a team that lives on in the collective memory of the Blaugrana fans. Although, if truth be told, that group, led by Ladislao Kubala, won three titles on the pitch and the other two without playing. They did not play the Copa Duarte (which is today the Spanish Super Cup), since they were both Liga and Copa del Rey champions, and the Copa Martini & Rossi was the cup given to the team that scored the most league goals. By contrast, Leo's Barça won all five cups on the pitch. All that remains is the FIFA Club World Cup, in December, to complete the set and break all the records. It will be the final chapter in the incredible Blaugrana saga.

But man cannot live on trophies and cups alone ... although, for Messi, football is very important. But first and foremost are his family, both present, and perhaps ... future. On this note, this year more than others, Leo has had his ups and downs. He has been extremely preoccupied with regard to the health of one family member (luckily everything has been resolved, it was a big scare and nothing more), but he has also been lucky enough to spend almost two months with his family. 'They were all here in Castelldefels, my uncles and aunts, my cousins, and it's always lovely when the house is full of family,' says Leo. And there's more: he has begun a romantic relationship. He admits to it on 25 January 2009 on *Hat Trik*, a Catalan TV programme. In front of the cameras, a boy asks him the most difficult question: 'Do you have a girlfriend?' And, after sticking out his tongue, he replies: 'I have a girlfriend and she's in Argentina. The truth is, I'm OK and I'm calm about it.' On 22 February, a month after his TV interview, he is seen in the streets of Sitges with his arm around a tanned girl with long hair. It kick-starts the race between the tabloids to find out the identity of the mystery girlfriend. She is the first official one after all the supposed squeezes attributed to him by the Argentine tabloids. Like the Rosario model Macarena

Lemos, before the 2006 World Cup, or eighteen-year-old Nerina, or the Argentine sex bomb Luciana Salazar.

Antonella Roccuzzo is a nineteen-year-old from Rosario, she is a Newell's fan, she studies nutrition and she is nothing like any of the fantasies concocted by the tabloids. 'I have known her since I was five, she is the cousin of my best friend (Luca Scaglia), and she's a Rosarina like me. I have seen her grow up and she has seen me grow up. Our families know each other, so I didn't have any doubts,' Leo tells Buenos Aires newspaper *Clarín* in May. He says that they have been in a relationship for a year. He has managed to keep it a secret because 'I'm discreet,' he says, adding: 'and if we hadn't decided to walk through Sitges during the carnivals, nobody would have known.' But the news is official and the two are photographed again in June in Buenos Aires, where Argentina are playing two qualifying matches for the South Africa World Cup. There is a family photo taken in the city streets, with Antonella arm-in-arm with Celia, Leo's mother. Marriage on the horizon?

No. 'I'm not getting married for the moment,' declares Leo. But the romance continues. We will wait … Leo has all he needs in order to keep both them and future generations comfortable: on 18 September 2009, he renews his contract with Barcelona for the fourth year running. He will receive more than 10 million euros a year – the highest amount for any Blaugrana footballer, and his buyout clause is increased from 150 to 250 million euros. A new contract that will terminate on 30 June 2016, when the Flea will be 29 years old. The future is guaranteed. All that is missing is the cherry on the cake of the happiest year of his life: the Ballon d'Or and the title of best player in the world. 'A dream. The best you can achieve as an individual,' as he says in an interview with L'Equipe TV. 'Who is your favourite for this year?' they ask him. 'I hope that this year it will be my turn.'

Chapter 36

Third time lucky

1, 19 and 21 December 2009

Yes – this time, it is his turn. This time, the saying 'third time lucky' comes true. After coming third in 2007 and second in 2008, Lionel Andrés Messi wins *France Football* magazine's 2009 Ballon d'Or. And he wins it by a mile – Messi gets 473 out of a possible 480 points, more than double the score of Cristiano Ronaldo, the runner-up, who is awarded 233 points. Xavi Hernandez comes in third with 173 points. Ninety of the award's 96 voters vote for Leo as their number one player; and with 98.54 per cent of the maximum number of points possible, nobody in the 54-year history of this prestigious prize has won it as convincingly or unanimously as Messi. Only Michel Platini, who won it in 1984 with 98.46 per cent of the possible points, has come close. It is a true triumph. According to the editor-in-chief of *France Football*, Denis Chaumier, there are three reasons for his success:

1. Messi's *coups de theatre*, his dribbling, his acceleration, his efforts to destabilise the opposition, his talent, his creative spirit and his sense of teamwork, along with some of his goals, have made a profound impression throughout the year. His influence within football is still not complete, but what I find marvellous is the fact that the sheer joy and impertinence of his

presence on the pitch resemble those of a certain Maradona.

2. We shouldn't forget that despite his young age, Messi has been among the contenders for the Ballon d'Or several times. Clearly, modern football will not give its highest honour to a flash in the pan, even one as impressive as Messi.

3. Messi is champion of Europe, of La Liga with Barcelona, winner of the European Super Cup and the Copa del Rey, and with the Argentine side has qualified for the final stages of the World Cup. It is hard to imagine a more remarkable run of achievements.

All sides are united in agreement on Messi's records, performances, talent, class and professional career. The journalists of *France Football*'s international voting panel have all bowed to the Flea. Tributes have poured in from around the world: from Japan to Iceland, from Ghana to New Zealand, from Kazakhstan to England. Describing his reasons for voting for Messi, the *Daily Telegraph* journalist Henry Winter writes in *France Football*:

Messi? Pure genius. He has a special relationship with the ball. He creates and scores goals, and works ceaselessly for the good of the team. To see him play is to witness a marvellous spectacle that greatly benefits the beautiful game.

It is 7.00pm on Monday 30 November 2009 when *France Football*'s representatives knock on the door of Messi's chalet in Castelldefels to deliver the good news. Leo has been awaiting this news with impatience and excitement, along with his girlfriend Antonella, his brother Rodrigo and his nephews and nieces. When the *France Football* director tells him that he has won the award he responds with his usual timid smile, but his eyes are sparkling.

The announcement comes at the end of a fantastic week for both Leo and Barça. On Tuesday 24 November, in the fifth match of the Champions League, the Blaugrana, with Piqué and Pedro, 'achieved an angelic victory over José Mourinho's Inter in a devilish match', in the words of *El País*. Up until now the task of getting into the last sixteen seemed a very difficult one for Guardiola's men, but now it is within their reach. Messi was unable to play in that match as he had sustained a muscular injury while playing Athletic Bilbao at San Mames on the final match day of La Liga, but on Sunday 29 November he is in the starting line-up for the classic derby against Cristiano Ronaldo's Real Madrid. This is the fourth time that the two superstars have met. The Portuguese player, who has been out of competition for more than 50 days, shows excellent form in the 66 minutes that he spends on the pitch. He leads the Madrid attack, but misses the best chance that the Whites get. His shot is turned away by Valdés, and for the fourth time he fails to score against Barça. Messi appears very little in the first half; he does not create play and his contribution is not decisive. He plays as a false forward but without his usual craftiness. However, in the second half, after Ibrahimović puts Barça ahead with an unstoppable left-foot shot and Busquets gets a red card, the Flea is once again at his best. He receives passes, brings others into play, asks questions of the Madrid defence, helps neutralise their attacks and invents two or three ingenious pieces of play. He contributes a great deal to the team just when they need it most. In the 88th minute he is in a position to make it 2-0. Alves crosses it into the centre from the right wing and Lionel shoots point-blank, which the incredible Casillas saves. It would have been a great pleasure for Messi to score his eighth goal against the Madrid keeper – his last one was a penalty in the friendly between Spain and Argentina on 14 November – but, as he says in his post-match interview, 'it was not to be, because of Casillas' great save. The most important thing is that Barcelona won.' And in reply to any questions about the Ballon d'Or, he replies: 'This afternoon Victor Valdés deserves the Ballon d'Or. He saved us.' This may be true, but Lionel has won his showdown with the 2008 winner of the award, Cristiano Ronaldo. The match was the perfect scenario for the baton to be passed on.

So, on this Monday in Castelldefels there is more than enough reason to celebrate. Wearing a green-and-white sweatshirt, Leo joins his family and the guests from *France Football* as they drink a toast to the boy who couldn't grow, and to his entry into the pantheon of world football. Afterwards, there is time to talk and to look at the front page – and 43 other pages – that the magazine has dedicated to this 'Young King of Football'.

The next day sees more front pages devoted to Messi, a huge press conference and interviews.

It is a time for reflection, for hearts on sleeves and for dedications. 'I cannot lie – I had a feeling that it could happen this year – but the results of the ballot surprised me,' says Messi in the Nou Camp press room. 'This prize is an honour; it is wonderful and very special, but I wasn't obsessed with winning it. I knew that if it was meant to happen it would, but either way I would keep on working in the same way as always,' he explains. Someone asks him how he feels about being the first Argentine player to win it. 'It's a great honour. Of course, under the modern rules Diego [Maradona] would have won it more than once – and Di Stéfano and Sivori both won it, albeit under different nationalities.' (We should remember that it is only since

1995 that the Ballon d'Or was opened up to any footballer who played for a European club, regardless of where he was from. Alfredo Di Stéfano, who was born in Buenos Aires, won it in 1957 and 1959 with Spanish nationality and Omar Sivori, who won it in 1961, did so with Italian nationality despite having been born in San Nicolás.)

And since Leo belongs to Barça as much as he does to Argentina, he does not forget how valuable the prize is to his 'home' team: 'The fact that I am the first footballer trained in the Barça youth academy to win this award really helps the "Barça project", and is very important for both the club and the people who work at the club.' As always, though, he thanks his family and his team-mates and dedicates the award to them. 'Without them, I would not have won it,' he says emphatically. He adds that if he had been on the voting panel, he would have voted for any of his team-mates: 'Xavi and Iniesta deserved this prize as well,' he says. He especially acknowledges Pep Guardiola, saying: 'The boss had a lot to do with it. I knew him from Barça B but had never had direct contact with him. I believe he is a very intelligent man with a huge knowledge of football, and that he has the ability to transmit this knowledge to others in the best possible way. He is a coach who recognises the human side of his players, and because of this they all love him. The titles we have won with him have been key to this award.'

The Barça coach replies: 'Leo is the rightful winner because as a player he is simply on another level. He has everything – he is tough, quick, scores goals even with his head [and who would dare to argue with this after the goal he scored in this way in the Champions League final?] – he understands the game and dominates all the records. But the difference with Leo is in his head, in his competitive spirit.'

And the boss is not the only one who is full of praise. On 1 December the whole world is talking about 'the boy who became a legend'.

The best footballer of 2009 is crowned on 6 December 2009 at 11.00am, on the set of the French football television programme *Télefoot*. This is where Denis Chaumier hands over the golden ball trophy in person. But the day before the ceremony, Messi has a match to play against Deportivo de La Coruña, in the Riazor stadium. The Flea celebrates his prize with two goals and some spectacular play. The spectators in the old Galician stadium shout 'Messi, Messi, Messi!' At midnight, after a 3-1 victory, Lionel goes into the changing room for a quick shower, as a private plane waits to take him to Paris Le Bourget airport. His flight lands in the French capital at 3.15am, and a car transports him to the Hotel George V in the eighth arrondissement. It's now 4.00am, but Lionel doesn't sleep; he spends the rest of the night listening to music (to be specific, Don Omar and DJ Flex), watching TV and chatting with his brothers Rodrigo and Matías and his sister, María Sol.

At 9.30am, the Parisian victory tour begins. Messi parades round the city, wearing a suit, tie and make-up, and stops in front of the Eiffel Tower before going into the television studio, where he is greeted by his former Barça team-mate Lilian Thuram. Then he is installed in front of the cameras for applause, speeches and finally the presentation of the trophy. After that there is a photo session with his family, friends and Barça president Joan Laporta, as well as people from the club, *France Football* and the French TV channel TF1. The official car picks him up and crosses Paris again, heading towards TF1's headquarters at Boulogne-Billancourt. But before Messi can have lunch in the Louis XIII salon of the Hotel George V and return home, he has to give one last press conference. It is now that Leo, sitting on a stool, confesses that he was a little bit impatient to receive the award, to lift the Ballon d'Or. Because six days can feel like a very long time. And he also surprises those present by admitting: 'I would love to win it again; it would be magnificent to win one more.'

Well, the boy has a lot of faith in himself, but we'll soon see. In the meantime, Barça have other challenges ahead. The first: ensuring they go through to the Champions League final sixteen. A very difficult match awaits Pep's men in Kiev. It is below zero degrees and Shevchenko and his team-mates are still convinced that they can go through. It's true that the Blaugrana have two useful results: they could lose by a goal or they could need to draw, depending on what happens at the Giuseppe Meazza in Milan where Inter and Rubin Kazan are playing at the same time as they are. But the main objective is to qualify first in the group to avoid the English superpowers: Chelsea, Manchester United and Arsenal. 'It's forbidden to speculate,' declares Guardiola, demanding that his players respect team etiquette and aim only for the victory. It will not be easy, because Dynamo go ahead after two minutes at the V. Lobanovskiy stadium, due to an error in the Catalan defence. Everything becomes complicated in the worst possible way: the 2008–09 champions are only one goal away from being knocked out. But Barça do not fall apart, they keep the ball from the Ukrainians, they push ahead without stopping, until they manage first to equalise (thanks to Xavi), and then to claim victory. It is sealed by Leo with a fantastic goal from a free kick. They have been pounding on Messi continually. He had the opportunity to equalise early on, but he wasn't able to take advantage of the bad clearance gifted to him by Shovkovskiy, and in the scuffle ended up losing his nerve in the area. Direct free kick in the 86th minute. It is the Flea who steps up to the ball: majestic execution, left-footed shot hammered into the back of the net. What a shame that four minutes later Almeida tackles him from behind – the ninth time he has been fouled – and he falls to the ground, injured.

'Anyone else in his situation could retire on the Ballon d'Or,' comments Pep Guardiola after the match. 'But Leo has an unmatched competitiveness in his soul, such ambition, that he gets angry and even in difficulty he wants another goal and he says: "I'm going for it." He goes right for it, straight ahead.'

The medical report states that Messi is suffering from a grade one sprain of his right ankle. He cannot play in the derby against Espanyol, and his participation in the semi-final of the Club World Cup in Abu Dhabi is threatened. On Saturday 12 December at the Nou Camp Leo is not playing, but he takes to the pitch to parade the Ballon d'Or in front of the 84,554 spectators. Celia, his mother, is there to present it to him.

An emotional moment and huge applause, before the long trip to Abu Dhabi, where Barça will face Mexican club Atlante in the semi-final on Wednesday 16 December, Atlante having just beaten Auckland City 3-0.

The photos and the TV footage from the United Arab Emirates show Messi on the beach, in blue swimming trunks and with a bandaged ankle, training in order to recover in good time. Leo and the whole of Barça are immersed in the competition, concentrating extremely hard on training in the lead-up to the game against Atlante, who are known as the Iron Colts. All predictions favour the Catalans far above the CONCACAF champions, but the Barça fans have not forgotten the two finals they lost in 1992 and 2006. They need to psych themselves up from the start. That's the plan, but things don't go their way. Barcelona are losing 1-0 after five minutes at the Zayed Sports City stadium. In the 35th minute Sergio Busquets equalises. Nonetheless Barça cannot handle Atlante. The Mexicans are defending well and they take advantage of the few opportunities they have, while the Blaugrana make fools of themselves and seem to lose the thread of the game. There is nothing to do but call on Messi. The Argentine, on the bench, was not planning to play unless absolutely necessary. But Barça have stalled, and Guardiola makes use of him in the 53rd minute. 'I knew that Messi was coming on judging by the screams from the crowd. I knew that his presence could upset the balance of the match,' Atlante manager José Cruz will say later, 'but I wasn't expecting him to do it so quickly.'

One minute, just one minute, is all it takes Leo to turn the match around and dictate the outcome. The Argentine manages to lose his marker while making a diagonal run, Ibrahimović sees him, spins around and offers him a beautiful and precise shot out deep. The Flea does the rest: perfect control, perfect sidestep around the Atlante goalie and, of course, perfect shot. The ball sputters forward into the net. It is his first touch, and it is 1-2; the Mexican resistance is over; Barça has woken up; Pedro nets the third, becoming the only footballer in history to have scored in six different club competitions in one season; now the eleven Blaugrana players can dedicate themselves to delighting the crowd with kicks and touches. Pure virtuoso. The chances come one after the other and Messi allows himself the luxury of missing another head-to-head with Vilar, the Argentine goalie, whom he knows well from the Albiceleste. And, once again, Messi has been the genie. José Cruz explains it as follows: 'Without Messi Barcelona is the best team in the world; when Leo plays they are from another galaxy.' There is nothing more to be said.

Only the final remains, on 19 December; only Estudiantes de La Plata, the Argentine team who have eliminated South Korean club Pohang Steelers 2-1 in the semi-final.

They are the team of the bald 'Brujita' ('little witch'), Juan Sebastián Verón, who was Leo's mentor in the 2007 Copa América, the globe-trotter who has become the team's central figure and dreams of repeating the achievements of his father Juan Ramón 'La Bruja' ('the witch') Verón. In 1968 the Estudiantes striker led the 'Rat Stabbers', as they are nicknamed, to victory in the Intercontinental Cup, beating Manchester United at Old Trafford.

It is certainly a dream given the forces on the pitch, but it lasts 89 minutes – almost the whole match, almost a miracle. The Argentines find the goal and the advantage towards the end of the first half (37th minute), with a clean header from Boselli, who finds a gap between Puyol and Abidal to finish Díaz's cross. Barça find themselves in the worst possible scenario: a goal down, no goals of their own, Messi with a yellow card to his name and, above all, a team that is lost and can find neither gaps in midfield, nor decisive passes. All the gaps are blocked by the Rat Stabbers' *trivote* (a formation of three defensive midfielders). Messi is invisible and Henry is nowhere to be found; Ibrahimović battles on with little effect.

By contrast, Estudiantes know exactly what to do: kill the game, block the ball and any initiative from the Barça players and recoil into their shell, not conceding even the slightest chance to their opponents, using all the tools at their disposal (fouls, clearances, letting the ball go out, substitutions, little kicks) to waste time, to get to the 90th minute and win the cup they so desire for the second time. Barça do not give up, they show all their strength of character, all their determination, they try again and again until Xavi gets it in the box in the final minutes. Piqué passes to Pedro who heads the ball, which collides with the net. They have equalised. Extra time. And Barça have won, the Argentines know it. Their faces say it all – they cannot hold up any more, they cannot stand up to little Messi, who plays as though he were playing in a playground; he scores with his chest, with his heart, with the emblem on his shirt. He anticipates his friend Juan Sebastián Verón, and in the 110th minute he finishes Daniel Alves' cross with that move which no one was expecting.

Why did he shoot with his chest instead of with his head? 'I was trying to play it safely. I saw that the goalie was unprepared,' Leo will explain the following day in an interview with *El País*. 'I thought it would be enough to put it in gently, just to the side of the area he was blocking. Luckily it turned out well.'

Simple as always, and as always the Flea looks up to the heavens and dedicates his goal to his grandmother Celia and to God for everything he has been given. After that there are only celebrations in the Blaugrana camp and tears from Pep Guardiola, who has been overtaken by emotion for once. Leo is the first to hug him and thank him, but he does not forget his opponents. He goes over to shake hands with all the Estudiantes players one by one, 'because they played fantastically, because they're Argentine, because they were very sad'. Third time lucky. After the 1992 and 2006 defeats, Barça win the trophy for the first time in the club's 110-year history. And the team are crowned kings of the world. No team has ever won six titles in one year. 'Right now I don't think we have fully realised what we have achieved,' confesses Messi to *El Periódico*. 'It will be difficult for another team to match this and, as time goes on, we will value it more and more.'

Barça have climbed to the top of the world, and Leo reaches the top once again on Monday 21 December in a snow-covered Zurich.

A few minutes after 9.00pm, UEFA president Michel Platini steps up to the podium accompanied by FIFA president Joseph 'Sepp' Blatter. Before he opens the golden envelope, one last look at the candidates for the prize. They roll the clip showing the faces of Cristiano Ronaldo, Andrés Iniesta, Kaká, Messi and Xavi.

Platini says he is very proud that all those nominated play in European teams. Then comes the most important moment, the announcement: 'The FIFA World Player 2009 is Lionel Messi.'

Third time lucky. Again. After coming second in 2007 and 2008, Leo is the number one. The Barça number 10 gets up from his seat, buttons his Ermenegildo Zegna jacket, adjusts his blue tie and goes up on stage. Michel Platini hands him the prize and invites him to speak.

> Good evening. First of all I would like to thank all the players who voted. It is a great honour for me to receive this prize, because it has been given by players from other clubs and other national teams, and that's really wonderful. I would like to thank – and share this with – my team-mates [here the camera pans to Iniesta in the audience], this is the best possible finish to what has been a magnificent year for Barcelona, for my team-mates, and for me. Thank you very much.

Leo's voice is shaking and he is smiling more than ever. He has won, and he has done it by a landslide once again: 1,073 points, three times as many as Cristiano Ronaldo, who is second with 352, Xavi is third (196), Kaká fourth (190) and Iniesta fifth (134). The managers and captains of 147 countries have awarded him an overwhelming victory.

'This is priceless, it's priceless,' declares Jorge Messi, who is accompanied by Celia, Matías, Rodrigo and María Sol. 'To win a prize, or for the team to win a title, those are things that are possible to comprehend. But to win everything at once, that was inconceivable,' says the Flea's father. And, quite emotional, he explains: 'It's the perfect end to a perfect year – more happiness would be impossible.'

'Planet Earth surrenders to Messi', say the headlines the following day, but it still remains for Leo to conquer the heart of one particular country; his country, Argentina. Because 'it annoys them that he still isn't a "Gardel" when it comes to the national team'. Moreover, because although they have qualified, with difficulty, for the South Africa World Cup, the Flea has never shone with the Albiceleste. 'Because in the Barcelona shirt he is transformed, and in the Argentine one he is not.' Yes, it's true, in Argentina they accuse him of a lack of affection towards his nation 'as if his lesser performance were due to a lack of motivation rather than the popularisation of a player who, with the Albiceleste, has more chance of winning the lottery than receiving a decent pass. Maradona has imposed a Messianic model,' writes David Gistau in *El Mundo,* 'in which Messi, the child of another time, does not fit; furthermore, he left Argentina very quickly – as if immersing himself in a kind of popular idolatry.' They do not realise that the problem does not lie with Messi, but rather with the team. They see him as a foreigner, they write 'Messi is not Argentine', because he has given all he can to Barça, he has given it his all in Europe and, what's more, he has ruined Estudiantes' dream, which was supported by practically the whole country. Yes, Messi has a problem with Argentines, or better, the Argentines have a problem with Messi. Leo knows it and it bothers him that they say that he does not care about the Albiceleste. And there is nothing that angers him more than when they say that he is not Argentine. 'What do they know about my feelings?' he exclaims. But this year the problem can be resolved. At the World Cup. All that is needed is for Leo to do what he does best.

Chapter 37

Barcelona

Present day

Twenty-two years are very few. The past is just over the shoulder, the future still seems far away. It is soon, too soon, to weigh things up and it is difficult to look forwards to see what the coming days will bring. But you can always try. Leo Messi agrees.

Sitting at a desk in a lounge in the bowels of the Nou Camp, he seems almost like a schoolboy who is about to do his homework in class. A mobile on the table is his only aide.

Let's begin.

What are the most difficult moments you have endured in your life?
'Moving country from Argentina to Spain. I left my hometown, my friends, my people. The first few years here were tough. There were times when my father and I were in Barcelona and the rest of the family was in Rosario. We were suffering. I missed Matías, Rodrigo, my little sister and my mother. I used to cry alone in my house so that my father wouldn't see.'

And the happiest moments?
'The titles I won with Barcelona and with Argentina.'

And the Ballon d'Or and the FIFA World Player 2009?
'The individual awards make the people I love happy, they make up for the sacrifices that my family has made. But the titles which make an entire town or country happy are worth much more. It's incredible, incomparable.'

But now you are the king of the world.
'No, I'm not, and I'm not the number one. I'm the same guy and I'm lucky to be part of a great team.'

Could you possibly have imagined a year like 2009?
'I would never have predicted all this. Not in my wildest dreams did I think that things would turn out so well.'

Let's go back to the past: what is your first good footballing memory?
'It was at the beginning, at Grandoli, we were playing in the Afi league against Amanecer. They said they were the best, the champions. My whole family was in the stands. And I scored four goals, one of which was very good.'

Why do you love football so much?
'I don't know. I first took a liking to it as a child, like all children do, and I still enjoy it a lot.'

How did you acquire such confidence with the ball, how did you learn all those tricks you know how to do?
'By spending every moment with a football. When I was little I would stand all on my own on a corner and kick the ball around continuously. But I don't study certain moves. I'm not like Ronnie [Ronaldinho], who practises a shot until it's perfect and he can do it in a match. I don't invent feints, or anything like that. I just play the way it comes out. I don't think about it.'

Who was the one who determined your love of football?
'My grandmother Celia took me to the ground the first time. She was a very important person, very special to all of us. She was such a good person. I remember Sundays at her house being something of a party. My brother Rodrigo and my cousin have been role models. And my father also supported me a lot.'

Has it been difficult to get to where you are today?
'All kids want to be footballers, but in order to make it you need to work hard and make a lot of sacrifices. And you have to go through some very tough times, like when I decided to stay in Barcelona ... It was my decision. No one forced me to make it. My parents asked me many times what I wanted to do. I wanted to stay in the youth academy because I knew that that was my chance to be a footballer. I was very responsible from a very young age.'

How have the growth problems and your height affected your development?
'I was a child, I didn't really have any idea of what was happening to me, apart from the injections in my legs every night. But, being smaller, I have learned to control the ball better on the ground, be more agile and faster than the bigger players in order to keep the ball.'

Which games throughout your career conjure up the best memories?
'That one against Chelsea in the Champions League three years ago, the derby against Real Madrid when I scored three goals and, of course, the final of the Under 20 World Cup and the semi-final against Brazil in Beijing.'

The most beautiful goals?
'If I had to choose now, I would say the one in Rome and the one against Estudiantes.'

And the one against Getafe?
'True, that one was also great.'

Is the one against Getafe the best goal you have scored in your life?
'Yes, it could be, but there were a couple of others when I was little, when I was ten or eleven years old and played for Newell's, which were similar. We have them on video at home.'

At around that age, when they asked you who your favourite player was, you responded: 'My brother Rodrigo and my cousin Maxi.' Have you ever had a football idol?
'No, I have never had a favourite player, or an idol. When I got a bit older I started to like Aimar, I admired his playing style. When I played against him at Valencia, I finally got to ask him for his shirt.'

And Maradona?
'He's the greatest.'

Did you see him play during his stint with Newell's in Rosario?
'I was very young, I was six years old. I went to a match the day that Maradona made his debut. But I don't remember it.'

Is it true that your father bought you a video of Maradona's best moments?
'I have seen Diego's goals many times, but I don't remember who gave me the video.'

*What do you make of it when everyone compares you with
Maradona and maintains that you're his successor?*
'It makes me very happy, because I still haven't done any-
thing, I need to keep growing and learning. Every day I
try to improve, to become a better footballer. And besides,
Diego is unique, there will never be another.'

It's the most obvious answer. Let's move onto another
topic.

What advice did Maradona give you?
'He told me to keep doing what I'm doing, always to enjoy
football and to look after myself, because it's a short career
and if you want to improve throughout it and make it last as
long as possible, you always have to be in good shape.'

And now, as the national team manager, what does he say to you?
'He gives me advice, he helps me. He always has things to
tell me.'

*Let's leave him aside and go back to the Getafe goal for a moment.
Some people say that that goal changed you. Is that true?*
'It could be that previously I played more respectfully, I was
more inhibited in front of my team-mates, and bit by bit I
was starting to go out there and play the way I like to play.'

*Everyone talks about the way you play … How would you define
it? Try to answer, even though it's a question you hate.*
'It's complicated talking about oneself, it's better to let others do the talking. What can I say? That I like to be behind
the strikers, create opportunities, find the goal whenever I
can.'

What is your best skill?
'Maybe my variation of pace.'

Another tiresome question: about tension. It seems strange that you virtually don't feel it.
'When I go onto the pitch I am not interested in the opposition, nor in who's marking me. I try to do well, enjoy myself and make a good contribution to my team.'

FC Barcelona?
'I have been here for nine years. I feel happy here. They took a chance on me when I was thirteen, I wanted to make it into the first team and I did. I wanted to win many titles with this team and I did. But I never forget that I am just one person, without the help of my team-mates I couldn't do anything.'

The Argentine team?
'Wearing the national shirt is something really great. Although I live thousands of miles away, I would like to be at all the games and bring a lot of happiness to my people.'

And what are your thoughts on the South Africa World Cup, after quite a difficult qualifying stage?
'One thing for sure is that the national team has experienced some tough moments: they cost us a lot, we suffered. We could see that we weren't doing as well as we could, they were pounding on us from all sides, it affected us a lot, whether we liked it or not. Now that we have qualified we have to find our game plan, our identity. We have some very good players and I think we'll succeed in being a force to be reckoned with at the World Cup. The most important thing is for the group to be fully united and not encounter any problems. We'll be fighting [for the title], I'm sure of it.'

Unfulfilled goal: would you like to play football in Argentina?
'I would enjoy playing for a club in my country. But that's a while away ...'

The telephone rings.
   Pause.
   It is a glorious day outside. Clear skies and an almost summery temperature, although according to the calendar it is winter. The grass gleams a shiny green. At the edge of the pitch, the tourists are taking a break in their tour of the stadium in order to pose for photos with life-size cardboard cutouts of their idols. A Japanese couple arrive. They choose Messi and she is delighted because she is the same height as him, she can put her arm around his neck. A group of schoolchildren appears, running wildly in and out around their favourite personalities. They all crowd around the cardboard Leo and Thierry Henry, although one of them claims a new idol: Bojan. The photographers, who can barely keep up with the demand, confirm that Messi is the most frequently requested.
   Inside, the phone call has finished. We can return to our conversation.

How do you find living with fame?
'I don't think about that. I think about being able to keep on playing, that's what I like the most. I live the same life as always. The only thing is that if I want to go out with my family in Rosario, I can't.'

Doesn't it bother you when people stop you in the street, asking for autographs, photos, kisses?
'No. There are people who spend hours waiting just to have a photo with me. It's only fair to give them some time.'

Is it true, as those who know you well say, that the fame has not gone to your head?
'It's true. I have my feet firmly on the ground and I never forget where I came from.'

And the money hasn't changed your life?
'It's the same as always. We're not people who waste money on luxury items.'

Do you like the advertising?
'I enjoy it, I like doing it.'

Changing the subject, let's talk about your first mentors.
'I learnt a lot from Guillermo Hoyos [his coach with the youth B team], he was very important to me. I did everything I could to move up the ranks.'

And your life mentors?
'My father, my family, my brother Rodrigo have always advised me and helped me in every way possible.'

You made a special dedication – 'I love you, Dad' – the day you scored your first goal on Argentine soil, at the Monumental stadium with the national team.
'I had promised, and he deserved it.'

What is your relationship like?
'Very good. We have spent a lot of time together here. We're mates, we're friends, although we have our ups and downs. Sometimes, he gets worried over little things, he starts to bother me and it annoys me ...'

Do you argue over contracts and investments?
'He always consults me, but he handles everything. I play the football.'

And what does your father think of the football?
'Ever since I was little, after a match, he tells me, "you played well" or "you played badly", but he doesn't get involved in the rest ...'

Aside from forging a brilliant career, your mother hopes that sooner or later you'll have a family.
'She's always telling me that. What matters to her is that I'm happy, but I'm still too young to think about having a family.'

But you have a girlfriend now?
'Yes.'
    He blushes tomato-red.

And what about the shyness?
'It's better, I've changed ...'

From whom do you get your bashfulness?
'Matías is like me, my dad also used to be like that ... My mother and Rodrigo are different ...'

What do you enjoy most in life aside from football?
'Being with my family and friends.'

Try to picture yourself in fifteen or twenty years' time. How do you see yourself?
'Living in Rosario with my family ... always close to my family.'

Family means everything to you, doesn't it?
'I owe a lot to my parents and my siblings. If they are OK, so am I.'

Let's take a test: here are some of the questions La Capital *asked you when you were thirteen years old. Let's see how you've changed. Favourite book?*
'Maradona's book (*Yo soy el Diego* [*I am the Diego*]), I started it but I never finished it. I'm not much of a reader ...'

Eight years ago you said the Bible. Are you religious?
'I don't practise, but I believe in God.'

Are you superstitious?
'No.'

Favourite CD?
'Argentine *cumbia* style music, but I don't know which group to choose.'

Favourite film?
'*El hijo de la novia* [*Son of the Bride*] and *Nueve reinas* [*Nine Queens*]. Ricardo Darín is my favourite actor. My grandmother looked a lot like the protagonist in *El hijo de la novia*, she used to do things that she also does and she also had Alzheimer's.'

Aims?
'To win many more titles.'

You really like winning.
'When you win it makes you happy, when you lose you always feel bad and you spend your time thinking about where and

how you went wrong. Ever since I was really little I have never liked to lose.'

A dream?
'To be world champion with Argentina.'

The phone rings again: it's Jorge, his father.

They are expecting him home for dinner. The whole family has come from Rosario: Celia, María Sol and his uncle and aunt, Claudio and Marcela.

In tracksuit trousers and a white hoodie with trainers, Leo Messi walks through the stadium hallway to the lift which leads to the car park. One last goodbye before he heads home, to his family.

I wonder what delicious things Celia and aunt Marcela have made today?

Career record

Personal summary
Full name: Lionel Andrés Messi
Place and Date of Birth: Rosario, Santa Fè, Argentina,
24 June 1987
Parents: Jorge and Celia
Sister: María Sol
Brothers: Matías and Rodrigo
Height: 169 cm
Weight: 67 kg

Early career
As a junior, played for Grandoli and Newell's Old Boys
in Rosario
At thirteen years old, scouted by Barcelona

Barcelona
First team debut: 16 November 2003 v FC Porto (away)
La Liga debut: 16 October 2004 v RCD Espanyol (away)
First goal: 1 May 2005, v Albacete (home)

Appearances (to end of 2008–09 season)
Liga 109 Goals 54
Copa del Rey 16 Goals 9
Europe 33 Goals 17

Argentina

Debut: 17 August 2005 v Hungary (away)

First goal: 1 March 2006 v Croatia (away)

Caps 41 Goals 13 (up to 14 November 2009)

Appearances

Under 20 World Cup 2005

World Cup 2006

Copa America 2007

Summer Olympics 2008

Honours won

Barcelona

FIFA Club World Cup 2009

European Super Cup 2009

Spanish Super Cup 2008–09

Champions League 2008–09

La Liga 2008–09

Copa del Rey 2008–09

Spanish Super Cup 2006–07

Champions League 2005–06

La Liga 2005–06

Spanish Super Cup 2005–06

La Liga 2004–05

Argentina national team

Under 20 World Cup 2005

Olympic gold medal, Beijing 2008

Individual honours

Ballon d'Or (European Player of the Year) 2009

FIFA World Player of the Year 2009

Onze d'Or 2009

Alfredo Di Stéfano trophy 2008–09

UEFA Champions League Top Scorer 2008–09

UEFA Club Forward of the Year 2008–09

UEFA Club Footballer of the Year 2008–09

LFP Best Player 2008–09

European Player of the Year (second place) 2008

FIFA World Player of the Year (second place) 2008

Under 21 European Footballer of the Year 2007

European Player of the Year (third place) 2007

FIFA World Player (second place) 2007

European FIFA Under 20 World Cup Top Scorer 2005

FIFA Under 20 World Cup Player of the Tournament 2005

Copa América Young Player of the Tournament 2007

Player of the Year, Argentina 2005, 2007

FIFPro Special Young Player of the Year 2006–07, 2007–08

FIFPro World Young Player of the Year 2005–06,
2006–07, 2007–08

World Soccer Young Player of the Year 2005–06,
2006–07, 2007–08

Premio Don Balón (Best Foreign Player in La Liga)
2006–07, 2008–09

EFE Trophy (Best Ibero-American Player in La Liga)
2006–07, 2008–09

FIFPro World XI 2006–07, 2007–08, 2008–09

Bibliography

Apo, Alejandro, *Y el fútbol contó un cuento* (Buenos Aires: Alfaguara, 2007)

Beha, Oliviero and Di Caro, Andrea, *Indagine sul calcio* (Milan: Bur, 2006)

Brera, Gianni, *Incontri e invettive* (Milan: Longanesi, 1974)

Fontanarrosa, Roberto, *Puro fútbol* (Buenos Aires: Ediciones de la Flor, 2000)

Frieros, Toni, *Leo Messi, el tesoro del Barça* (Barcelona: Edecasa, 2006)

Galdeano, Arnau, *Estimat Messi* (Barcelona: Empúries, 2007)

Galeano, Eduardo, *El fútbol a sol y sombra* (Madrid: Siglo XXI de España Editores, 1995)

Grosso, Cristian, *Futbolistas con historia(s)* (Buenos Aires: Ediciones Al Arco, 2007)

Hugo, Víctor and Perfumo, Roberto, *Hablemos de fútbol* (Buenos Aires: Planeta, 2006)

Luque, Xavier and Finestres, Jordi, *El caso Di Stéfano* (Barcelona: Península, 2006)

Maradona, Diego Armando, *Yo soy el Diego* (Barcelona: Planeta, 2001)

Sebreli, Juan José, *La era del fútbol* (Buenos Aires: Debolsillo, 2005)

Toro, Carlos, *Anécdotas del fútbol* (Madrid: La Esfera de los Libros, 2004)

Valdano, Jorge, *El miedo escénico y otras hierbas* (Madrid: Aguilar, 2002)

Vargas, Walter, *Fútbol Delivery* (Buenos Aires: Ediciones Al Arco, 2007)

Magazines
El Gráfico, Buenos Aires
Don Balón, Barcelona

Newspapers
Spain
El País
El Mundo
La Vanguardia
El Periódico de Catalunya
Marca
As
Sport
Mundo Deportivo

Argentina
La Nación
Clarín
Época
Olé
La Capital

UK
The Times
Guardian

Italy
Corriere della Sera
Gazzetta dello Sport
Corriere dello Sport

Yearbooks
Guía de la Liga 2005 (*Marca* Magazines)
Guía de la Liga 2006 (*Marca* Magazines)

Guía de la Liga 2007 (*Marca* Magazines)
Guía de la Liga 2008 (*Marca* Magazines)
Guía de la Liga 2009 (*Marca* Magazines)
Guía de la Liga 2010 (*Marca* Magazines)

TV channels
Canal +
TyC
Fox TV
TV3

Websites
www.fifa.com
www.uefa.com
www.afa.com.ar
www.gloriosonewells.com.ar
www.nob.com.ar
www.rosariocentral.com
www.fcbarcelona.com
www.youtube.com
www.lionelmessi.org
www.liomessi.wordpress.com
www.messiadictos.com

Acknowledgements

Thanks to Leo Messi and to his family: Jorge, Celia, Rodrigo and Marcela.

And, in order of appearance, thanks to Laure Merle d'Aubigné, Bernat Puigtobella, Fèlix Riera, Montserrat Molons, Marcela Martínez, Claudio Martínez, Julio Lagos, Diego Torres, Fernando Solanas, Asier del Horno, Pablo Zabaleta, Hugo Tocalli, Pancho Ferraro, Carlos Garaycochea, Carlos Bilardo, Manuel Giménez, Dolores García, Fernando Niembro, Claudio Codina, Mariano Bereznicki, Diego Schwarzstein, Cintia Arellano, Salvador Aparicio, Ernesto Vecchio, Adrián Coria, Horacio del Prado, Roberto Perfumo, Alfio Basile, Santiago Segurola, Cristina Cubero, José Miguel Terés, Gianluca Zambrotta, Alex García, Charly Rexach, Josep Maria Minguella, Horacio Gaggioli, Frank Rijkaard, Jorge Valdano, Ton Vilalta Seco, Albert Torrescasana, Ignacio Iraola, Analía Romano, Oliver Pugh, Simon Flynn, Andrew Furlow, Nick Sidwell, Sarah Higgins, Najma Finlay and Sheli Rodney.

Dedicated to Elvira, for everything she has done and continues to do. To Lorenzo, Olmo, Alda and Tullio.